The Dictionary of
Educational
Terms

The Dictionary of
Educational
Terms

David Blake & Vincent Hanley

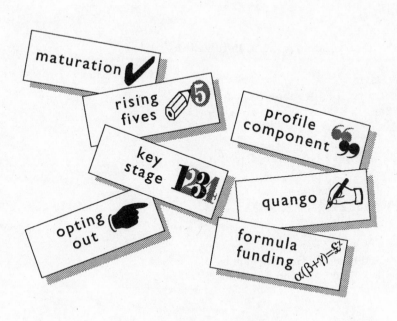

arena

Published by
Arena
Ashgate Publishing Limited
Gower House
Croft Road
Aldershot
Hants
GU11 3HR
England

Ashgate Publishing Company
Old Post Road
Brookfield
Vermont 05036
USA

British Library Cataloguing in Publication Data

Blake, David
  Dictionary of Educational Terms
  I. Title II. Hanley, Vincent
  370.3

Library of Congress Catalog Card Number: 95-77012

ISBN 1 85742 253 8 (paperback)
ISBN 1 85742 256 2 (hardback)

Printed and bound in Great Britain by
Hartnolls Limited, Bodmin, Cornwall

ACRONYMS

AAU	Academic Audit Unit
ACAC	Curriculum and Assessment Authority for Wales
ACC	Association of County Councils
ACE	Advisory Centre for Education
ACFHE	Association of Colleges for Further and Higher Education
ACPC	Area Child Protection Committee
ACRG	Access Course Recognition Group
AEO	Area Education Officer
AFC	Association for Colleges
ALBSU	Adult Literacy and Basic Skills Unit
AMA	Association of Metropolitan Authorities
AMG	Annual Maintenance Grant
AMMA	Assistant Masters' and Mistresses' Association
APU	Assessment of Performance Unit
APVIC	Association of Sixth Form Colleges
AT	attainment target
ATCDE	Association of Teachers in Colleges and Departments of Education
ATL	Association of Teachers and Lecturers
ATTI	Association of Teachers in Technical Institutions
AUT	Association of University Teachers
AVA	Authorised Validation Agencies
BA	Bachelor of Arts
BAAS	British Association for the Advancement of Science
BEd	Bachelor of Education
BEI	British Education Index
BTEC	Business and Technology Education Council
CASE	Campaign for the Advancement of State Education
CATE	Council for the Accreditation of Teacher Education
CATS	Credit Accumulation and Transfer Scheme
CCW	Curriculum Council for Wales
CDT	craft, design and technology
CEO	Chief Education Officer

CERI	Centre for Educational Research and Innovation
CEWC	Council for Education in World Citizenship
CGLI	City and Guilds of London Institute
CLEA	Council of Local Education Authorities
CNAA	Council for National Academic Awards
CPS	Centre for Policy Studies
CPVE	Certificate of Pre-Vocational Education
CSV	Community Service Volunteers
CSYS	Certificate of Sixth Year Studies
CTC	City Technology Colleges
CVCP	Committee of Vice-Chancellors and Principals
CSE	Certificate in Secondary Education
DENI	Department of Education Northern Ireland
DES	Department of Education and Science
DFE	Department for Education
DipHE	Diploma of Higher Education
DT	design and technology
DTI	Department of Trade and Industry
DVE	Diploma of Vocational Education
EA	Education Association
EBD	emotional and behavioural difficulties
EFL	English as a foreign language
EIS	Educational Institute of Scotland
EIU	Economic and Industrial Understanding
EKSS	end of key stage statements
EOC	Equal Opportunities Commission
ERA	Education Reform Act
ERIC	Educational Resources Information Centre
ESG	Education Support Grant
ESN	educationally subnormal
ESOL	English for speakers of other languages
ESRC	Economic and Social Research Council
EWO	Education Welfare Officer
EWS	Education Welfare Service
FAS	Funding Agency for Schools
FE	further education
FEFC	Further Education Funding Council
FEU	Further Education Unit
FT	full-time
FTE	full-time equivalent
GCE	General Certificate of Education
GCSE	General Certificate of Secondary Education
GEST	Grants for Education Support and Training

GMS	grant maintained schools
GNVQ	General National Vocational Qualification
GPDST	Girls' Public Day School Trust
GSA	Girls' Schools Association
GSB	General Schools Budget
GTC	General Teaching Council
HE	higher education
HEFCE	Higher Education Funding Council England
HEQC	Higher Education Quality Council
HMC	Headmasters' Conference
HMCI	Her Majesty's Chief Inspector of Schools
HMI	Her Majesty's Inspectorate
HoD	head of department
HoF	head of faculty
IAPS	Incorporated Association of Preparatory Schools
IIEP	International Institute for Educational Planning
ILEA	Inner London Education Authority
INSET	in-service education and training
IQ	intelligence quotient
ISIS	Independent Schools Information Service
IT	information technology
KS	key stage
LEA	local education authority
LMS	local management of schools
MA	Master of Arts
MEd	Master of Education
MSC	Manpower Services Commission
NAGC	National Association for Gifted Children
NAGM	National Association for Governors and Managers
NAHT	National Association of Headteachers
NAME	National Anti-Racist Movement in Education
NAPE	National Association for Primary Education
NASD	National Association for Staff Development
NAS/UWT	National Association of Schoolmasters/Union of Women Teachers
NATE	National Association for the Teaching of English
NATFHE	National Association of Teachers in Further and Higher Education
NCB	National Children's Bureau
NCC	National Curriculum Council
NCES	National Centre for Educational Standards
NCET	National Council for Educational Technology
NCPTA	National Confederation of Parent–Teacher Associations

NCVQ	National Council for Vocational Qualifications
NEC	National Extension College
NEF	New Education Fellowship
NFER	National Foundation for Educational Research
NIACE	National Institute of Adult Continuing Education
NNEB	National Nursery Examination Board
NQT	newly-qualified teacher
NRA	National Record of Achievement
NSG	non-statutory guidance
NUS	National Union of Students
NUT	National Union of Teachers
NVQ	National Vocational Qualifications
OFSTED	Office for Standards in Education
OHMCI	Office of Her Majesty's Chief Inspector of Schools
ONC	Ordinary National Certificate
OND	Ordinary National Diploma
ORACLE	Observational Research and Classroom Learning Evaluation
OU	Open University
PAT	Professional Association of Teachers
PC	profile component
PCAS	Polytechnics Central Admissions System
PGCE	Postgraduate Certificate of Education
PIs	performance indicators
PoS	programme of study
PPG	pre-school playgroup
PRP	performance related pay
PSE	personal and social education
PTA	Parent–Teacher Association
PTR	pupil–teacher ratio
QTS	qualified teacher status
ROSLA	Raising of the School Leaving Age
RSA	Royal Society of Arts
SACRE	Standing Advisory Council on Religious Education
SATs	standard assessment tasks
SCAA	School Curriculum and Assessment Authority
SCE	Scottish Certificate of Education
SCEA	Service Children's Education Authority
SCIP	Schools Council Industry Project
SCITT	School-Centred Initial Teacher Training
SDP	school development plan
SEAC	Schools Examination and Assessment Council
SEN	special educational needs

SEO	Society of Education Officers
SHA	Secondary Heads Association
SLA	School Library Association
SLS	School Library Service
SNS	standard national scale
SOA	statements of attainment
SOED	Scottish Office Education Department
SRC	Science Research Council
SSA	standard spending assessment
SSR	staff–student ratio
SSRC	Social Science Research Council
STA	specialist teacher assistant
STABIS	State Boarding Information Service
STOPP	Society of Teachers Opposed to Physical Punishment
TA	teacher assessment
TECs	Training and Enterprise Councils
TGAT	Task Group on Assessment and Testing
TOPS	Training Opportunities Scheme
TTA	Teacher Training Agency
TVEI	Technical and Vocational Education Initiative
U3A	University of the Third Age
UCAS	Universities and Colleges Admissions Service
UCCA	Universities Central Council on Admissions
UCLU	University and College Lecturers' Union
UDE	university department of education
UNESCO	United Nations Educational, Scientific and Cultural Organisation
VSO	Voluntary Service Overseas
WEA	Workers' Education Association
WOED	Welsh Office Education Department
YTS	Youth Training Scheme

~ A ~

A level *GCE* A level (advanced) examinations are taken by candidates after a course of two years (or less through intensive courses). The conventional academic requirement for admission to *university* is a minimum of two passes at A level in suitable subjects. See *mock examination; Scottish Certificate of Education (SCE); S level.*

ability The term is freely used but is difficult to define. Its general use assumes that individuals possess innate or acquired powers of learning in academic or technical spheres. Some educationalists believe that *aptitude* rather than ability may be a better term for specific uses (e.g. in technology) but many use the terms interchangeably. However, it would be wrong to assume a straightforward equivalence between ability and *attainment*; it is possible that a learner's attainment may fall below expectations for his or her level of ability. See *gifted children; halo effect; intelligence; skill.*

Abitur The Abitur is the German equivalent of *A levels* in the UK but there is one important difference. A levels are narrowly based and concentrate on specialising in depth; the Abitur, much like the French *baccalauréat*, is broad-based and is the culmination of secondary education in breadth.

Academic Audit Unit (AAU) The Unit, established in 1989 by the *Committee of Vice-Chancellors and Principals* (CVCP), was located at the University of Birmingham. It was concerned with academic *standards*, ways in which they are *monitored* and dissemination of *information* about successful work. In 1992, the Unit and *CNAA* were replaced by the *Higher Education Quality Council* (HEQC) as a result of the *Further and Higher Education Act (1992).*

academic board The board is a committee of academics, the function of which is to oversee the academic work of a college or university. Some members are elected; others are ex officio. In some institutions the board is directly responsible to *governors*.

academic disciplines   The disciplines are bodies or areas of *knowledge* – e.g. mathematics, history – within which teaching, learning and research may be focused in schools, colleges and universities.

accent   See *Standard English*.

access course   This is a route into *higher education* for students who do not hold the conventional, standard qualifications of *A levels* (i.e. in a minimum of two subjects). Students who achieve the necessary levels in access courses may be offered places by *universities* or colleges. Access courses may be taught by appropriate colleges of *further education* or universities. See *Higher Education Quality Council (HEQC); mature students; open admission; university entrance requirements*.

Access Course Recognition Group (ACRG)   In 1989, the *Council for National Academic Awards* (CNAA) and the *Committee of Vice-Chancellors and Principals* (CVCP) set up the ACRG to deal with issues concerning parity and recognition of access courses on a national basis. In practice, the ACRG grants powers of approval for courses to Authorised Validation Agencies (AVA), i.e. specific colleges and *universities*. Approval may be granted after a process of validation in which courses are considered for their appropriateness as alternative preparation for entry into *higher education*.

accountability   Accountability is a business efficiency notion that became popular in the educational world in America in the 1960s and spread to other countries in which governments were seeking ways to examine spending and other responsibilities for education. Accountability, therefore, is rooted in widespread concern about such matters as financing, provision, management and curriculum. Educationalists have drawn attention to different facets of accountability. Some emphasise standards, parental participation, curriculum entitlement and provision; others point to teachers' contractual, moral and professional obligations. Since the *Education Reform Act (1988)*, priority has been given to ways of publicly ensuring accountability; schools are required to publish examination and *National Curriculum assessment* results and *league tables* of schools' performances are compiled. In addition, *performance indicators* (PIs) based on *truancy* rates, numbers of pupils of post-compulsory age staying on in school/college and statistics for leavers' first destinations are seen by government as legitimate measures for accountability despite unease in some quarters about the emphasis on outputs. See *efficiency (of school); information; Parents' Charter*.

accreditation   This is the set of formal procedures through which one academic body or university accredits the awards of another and acts as guarantor of appropriate *standards*. See *credit; Credit Accumulation and Transfer Scheme (CATS)*.

action research   This kind of research is not confined to education; it can be adopted in a variety of social settings, e.g. hospitals, prisons, youth clubs. When following the action research approach, the researcher studies a specific social situation in order to understand what is actually happening and, in the light of findings, to introduce improvements. It is an approach much valued by teachers and schools as a tool for professional development and improvement of practice.

active learning   In this kind of *learning*, learners are encouraged to participate in active ways. Thus, they demonstrate involvement by doing, making or constructing (on their own initiative) through their own understandings and meanings and do not simply learn by *rote*, memorise and regurgitate facts. See *passive learning*.

admission   All *maintained* primary *schools* must admit pupils on demand up to the school's *standard number*. All maintained secondary schools must admit pupils up to either their standard number or to any higher number which may have been fixed. An order to increase a standard number may be made on the application of either the *LEA* or its governing body to the *Secretary of State*.

Parents must send their children to school at the beginning of the term following the child's fifth birthday. Where space allows, some LEAs will admit pupils in the term before their fifth birthdays. These pupils are known as *rising fives*.

The policy of *open enrolment* is designed to give parents more choice over the schools they wish their children to attend. In practice there is less choice than the term implies; where a school is very popular it will normally give the vast majority of places to children living nearby (in the school's *catchment area*). If parents wish to send their children to a school other than their local school the permission of the LEA is required. This can be time-consuming and difficult. In practice, the determining factor is the availability of a place in the selected school (as well as the ability of parents to find transport to get children to school). There are appeals regulations for parents who are dissatisfied with the admissions procedures. See *non-selective schools; Parents' Charter; selective schools.*

adult education   A wide range of interests is catered for in adult education. There is provision for many kinds of leisure pursuits and study leading to recognised qualifications and *degrees.*

Following the *Further and Higher Education Act (1992),* the government distinguished between vocational and non-vocational courses. The *Further Education Funding Council* (FEFC) now finances vocational courses (also referred to as schedule 2 courses) and *local education authorities* are responsible for leisure programmes. It has been estimated that 3.5 million adults are attracted to courses each year. Courses are conducted in community centres, further education colleges, LEA centres, university departments and through *distance learning,* e.g. Open University. See *adult literacy; continuing education; evening classes; mature students; National Extension College (NEC); National Institute of Adult Continuing Education (NIACE); open learning; University of the Third Age (U3A).*

adult literacy   The low level of *literacy* skills of a significant number of adults was officially acknowledged in 1975 when the Adult Literacy Research Agency was established. Schemes were devised to alleviate the problem and special units to monitor and advise were set up. In 1980 the Adult Literacy and Basic Skills Unit (ALBSU) was set up. For further information contact:

Adult Literacy and Basic Skills Unit (ALBSU)
Commonwealth House
1–19 New Oxford Street
London
WC1A 1NU

Telephone No: 0171 405 4017

Advanced Supplementary GCE (AS)   This new examination was intended to broaden the curriculum in the sixth form. AS courses maintain A level standards but contain only half the content of the full A level course. Instead of following full courses in three subjects, students can follow two A levels *and* two AS courses as well. See *GCE.*

Advisory Centre for Education (ACE)   The Advisory Centre for Education was founded in 1960 to act as a consumers' association for education. It gives free advice to parents and publishes an informative bulletin. For further information contact:

Advisory Centre for Education (ACE)
16 Aberdeen Studios
22 Highbury Grove
London
N5 2EA

Telephone No: 0171 354 8321

advisory teacher This category of teacher is appointed or sec-
onded to an *LEA*'s advisory team to provide advice and support for
teachers in a subject or cross-curricular area. Many work closely with
advisers and lead *in-service* courses. Since the introduction of *local
management of schools* (LMS) and further delegation of in-service funding to schools, LEAs have been reducing the number of advisory
teachers.

after-school activities Schools and teachers often pride themselves on the range of clubs, societies and activities offered after
school. Teachers' involvement is usually voluntary and unpaid. See
extended day; extra-curricular activities.

age of transfer The age at which primary pupils move from *primary* to *secondary* school is the age of transfer. In most cases, the age of
transfer is 11, the year in which *Key Stage* 2 finishes and Key Stage 3
begins, but there may be variations to accord with local patterns of
schooling. See *junior school; middle school; transition.*

aggregation This term is used in *assessment.* It is the process or
device through which the results of different assessments are brought
together to produce an overall result. Thus, levels within *attainment
targets* in the *National Curriculum* can be aggregated for reporting on
profile components.

agreed syllabus The agreed syllabus was the *syllabus* for religious
education which the 1944 Education Act required local education
authorities to establish. The syllabus had to be non-denominational. It
was drawn up with teachers and church representatives advising
local education authorities.

allowance Teachers' salaries used to be categorised on various
scales, leading to the ownership of a scaled post for jobs carrying particular responsibilities. Responsibility allowances were sometimes
called incentive allowances, denoting that payment above the norm

was thought to lead to enhanced *performance*. A teacher's salary is now located at a certain point on the 17-point pay spine for classroom teachers. See *standard national scale (SNS)*.

alternative education   See *exclusion; free school; home education; small schools.*

ancillary staff   These are non-teacher members of staff who assist in a school or college. The term is now applied widely to include secretaries, librarians, technicians, caretakers, cleaners, cooks and *welfare assistants*. Welfare assistants are sometimes called *classroom assistants* in England and Wales; in Scotland, they are known as auxiliaries. See *support staff.*

Annual Maintenance Grant (AMG)   The AMG is the yearly grant made to *grant maintained schools*. The grant is intended to cover normal running costs and is topped up by a further sum in respect of certain services which the schools previously received from their *LEAs*.

appraisal   Staff appraisal is now a requirement in all schools. It was for some time a hotly contested aspect of educational policy, with fears expressed by teacher trade unions that an appraisal might be unfair, especially if linked to *performance related pay* and promotion. There were some well-publicised pilot schemes, for example in Suffolk, which began to explore some of the practical issues surrounding appraisal. A number of approaches to appraisal are possible; for example it is possible to include a strong element of peer appraisal, on the one hand, or to see it as part of a more hierarchical line-management approach on the other. Systems of staff appraisal commonly involve a review of the previous year's professional activity and the setting of agreed targets for professional activity in the year to come. It is believed by some that a beneficial approach to staff appraisal in education is one which views practitioners as a part of staff teams and encourages a self-evaluative, self-critical approach to professional performance. Evidence is beginning to emerge that appraisal systems which are directly related to financial rewards can lead to engagement in the process at only a superficial level and to compliance or going through the motions. In the best-run schemes there is a strong emphasis on *staff development* for the appraisers.

appropriate authority   Under the Education (Schools) Act 1992, the appropriate authority for *maintained schools* (other than *GM* *schools*) whose governing bodies do not have delegated budgets is the *LEA*. The proprietors of schools, City Technology Colleges and city colleges for technology and the arts are the appropriate authorities approved by the Secretary of State under Section 11(3)(a) of the Education Act 1981. In all other cases, the schools' governing bodies are the appropriate authorities.

aptitude   Aptitude is normally used to indicate latent powers of *learning* or, as many teachers interpret it, potential. Aptitude tests can be used sometimes to measure the extent to which *knowledge* and *skills* might be acquired in particular curriculum or vocational areas. See *ability; differentiation*.

Area Child Protection Committee (ACPC)   These are committees of local Social Services departments. For information, contact Social Services in the local telephone directory. See *child protection*.

Area Education Officer (AEO)   The AEO is the officer of the *LEA* who is responsible for the education service in a particular area of the county. He or she is responsible to the County Education Officer for overseeing the implementation of policy, the operation of the service in the area and for dealing with parents' enquiries or *complaints* not satisfied at school level.

articled teacher   This is a *graduate* who undertakes a school-based *PGCE* course of two years under the aegis of an approved *teacher training* institution. Students spend 80 per cent of the time in schools working with *mentors* and 20 per cent in the institution where they follow professional courses. *Bursaries* are paid in each year and, if successful, students gain *Qualified Teacher Status (QTS)*.

assembly   The term is generally used to denote the gathering of all the children in a school for a communal event, normally the school's act of collective worship. Because of the size of some schools, assemblies sometimes take place with particular groups of children, for example children in the lower school or in year groups.

assessment   A key part of the teachers' role is to make sound assessments of pupils' *learning*. This involves a judgement about the quality of a pupil's work and the level at which a pupil is operating. Assessment normally involves judgement of an individual's written work, but it may also involve judgements about projects, performance, oral presentations and group performance. Under the *National*

Curriculum, tests are in place to help arrive at an assessment of pupil performance at the end of each *key stage*. Assessment may be *norm-* or *criterion-referenced* and *formative* or *summative*. A fundamental purpose of assessment is the diagnosis of pupil learning to help plan succeeding teaching episodes. Mention is sometimes made of *ipsative assessment*, an idea where the individual defines certain assessment objectives within a broad framework, thus leading to a more individualised learning programme. It is generally agreed that teachers and learners benefit from the existence of explicit assessment criteria, guidelines which explain what performance is necessary in order to achieve specified *grades*. See *aggregation; attainment; attainment test; continuous assessment; examining; item; levels of attainment; multiple choice test; performance test; practical assessment; profile component (PC); reports; School Curriculum and Assessment Authority (SCAA); Schools Examination and Assessment Council (SEAC); Task Group on Assessment and Testing (TGAT); teacher assessment (TA); teachers' ratings; testing; weighting*.

Assessment of Performance Unit (APU)   The work of the Unit petered out as the *National Curriculum* became more established. Having been set up in 1974 by the *Department of Education and Science* (DES) to monitor and assess achievement in seven areas – scientific, aesthetic, language, modern languages, physical, social and personal, and mathematics – the Unit was eventually responsible for testing performance of 11 and 15-year-olds in mathematics, English, science and foreign languages only.

assistant   Assistants are *undergraduates* or *postgraduates* from other countries who are engaged by *LEAs* or *secondary schools* to provide the expertise of native speakers in the teaching of foreign languages. See *language support teacher*.

Assistant Masters' and Mistresses' Association (AMMA)   See *Association of Teachers and Lecturers (ATL)*.

Assisted Places Scheme   This scheme was introduced in 1980 and was intended to assist pupils from low-income groups to enter private education. Funded by the government, the scheme provides funding for all or part of fees for secondary pupils who gain places at certain *independent schools*. The schools may set tests and interview prospective pupils. Boarding costs are not included in the award. See *entrance awards*. For further information contact:

Department for Education (DFE)
Mowden Hall
Darlington
DR3 9BG

Telephone No: 01325 460155

Welsh Office Education Department (WOED)
Government Buildings
Ty Glas Road
Llanishen
Cardiff
CF4 5WE

Telephone No: 01222 761456

Scottish Office Education Department (SOED)
Room 4/14 New St Andrew's House
St James's Centre
Edinburgh
EH1 3SY

Telephone No: 0131 556 8400

Association for Colleges (AFC)   The AFC is a comparatively new association for *further education* colleges. It represents colleges which in the recent past may have belonged to the Tertiary Colleges Association, the Association of Colleges for Further and Higher Education (ACFHE), the Association of Principals, the Further Education Campaign Group or the Association of Sixth Form Colleges (APVIC) – all of which were incorporated when the new association was established. See *higher education; sixth form college; tertiary college*. For further information contact:

Association for Colleges
344–354 Gray's Inn Road
London
WC1X 8BP

Telephone No: 0171 833 1933

Association of County Councils (ACC)   The ACC is concerned with government and public services at county level and represents councils in high-level discussions with central government and parliamentary committees. The focus of interest is usually, but not exclusively, finance; as an employer's group, the Association is also involved in negotiating pay and conditions with trade *unions*. See *Council of Local Education Authorities (CLEA)*. For further information contact:

Association of County Councils (ACC)
Eaton House
661A Eaton Square
Westminster
London
SW1W 9BH

Telephone No: 0171 235 1200

Association of Metropolitan Authorities (AMA) The AMA monitors central government's plans and legislative programmes, as they impinge on authorities' duties and responsibilities, and keeps members informed. In addition, it represents authorities' views in discussion with central government and parliamentary committees. The Association has watchdog committees to advise it on particular areas e.g. education, social services. See *Council of Local Education Authorities (CLEA)*. For further information contact:

Association of Metropolitan Authorities (AMA)
35 Great Smith Street
Westminster
London
SW1P 3BJ

Telephone No: 0171 222 8100

Association of Teachers and Lecturers (ATL) Formerly the *Assistant Masters and Mistresses Association* (AMMA), ATL was the new title adopted in 1993. It attracts members from schools and further education colleges, is not politically aligned with any party and does not belong to the Trades Union Congress. See *unions*.

Association of University Teachers (AUT) The AUT, founded in 1909, can claim membership of the majority of lecturers in *universities* and certain others engaged in administrative work. The association is concerned especially with salaries and contractual and professional issues. For further information contact:

Association of University Teachers (AUT)
United House
Pembridge Road
London
W11 3JY

Telephone No: 0171 221 4370

attainment   Attainment is best understood as the level of *learning* or mastery of *knowledge* or *skills* achieved to date in certain areas. Proof of achievement can only be verified by collecting evidence e.g. demonstrations of skills, *assessment*. Unlike attainment, *aptitude* refers more specifically to learners' potential, i.e. latent ability to master skills or knowledge in the future. See *levels of attainment; performance test; profile; statement of attainment (SOA)*.

attainment targets (ATs)   These targets are objectives for knowledge, skills and understanding in both core and foundation subjects. Pupils of different abilities and maturities are expected to develop them during the course of their education. See *levels of attainment; National Curriculum; profile component (PC); programme of study (PoS); statement of attainment (SOA)*.

attainment test   This kind of test is intended to measure *learning* to date in a particular curriculum area or skill. See *attainment*.

attendance   Under current legislation, children must attend school from the age of five, i.e. from the beginning of the term following the fifth birthday. The age at which they may leave is 16; those who reach 16 between September and January can leave at the end of the Spring term and those who have birthdays after January can leave at the end of May. Attendance registers in which pupils are marked present or absent at the beginning of each morning and afternoon session must be kept. Schools are required to distinguish between authorised and unauthorised absences. Rates of unauthorised absence must be shown in annual reports and *prospectuses*. Subject to certain safeguards concerning corrections and preservation, schools may retain attendance records and registers on computers. See *league tables; performance indicators* (PIs); *truancy*.

Attendance Order   This is an order, issued by a court, in which parents or guardians are required to ensure regular attendance at school by their children. In ordinary circumstances, parents are responsible for ensuring that children attend *a* school but, under an Attendance Order, the pupil concerned must attend the particular school named in the order.

attitude   An attitude is manifested through patterns of settled behaviour or habitual reactions and is an extremely important factor in *learning*. See *skill*.

Audit Commission   The Commission, funded by the government, is independent and acts accordingly in its close examinations of the financing of public services. Its reports pinpoint weaknesses and strengths in the services' effectiveness and help to make them publicly accountable.

aural   This term is often used for matters concerning listening and learning, especially in the teaching of pupils whose learning is impaired. See *learning difficulty*.

autism   Researchers are still uncertain about the causes of autism, a condition in which children are isolates and do not communicate satisfactorily with peers or parents. Autistic children may try to avoid change and may follow repetitious patterns of behaviour. Although some may have high *intelligence quotients* (IQs), it is inevitable that *attainment* will be below average. However, in a small number of documented and well-publicised cases, autistic children have demonstrated exceptional ability in narrow areas, e.g. feats of memory, detailed drawing. There is now a general belief that teaching methods for this group of pupils are improving. See *learning difficulty*.

auxiliaries   See *ancillary staff*.

~ B ~

baccalauréat This examination is taken by French pupils before leaving school at 17 or 18. There are three types, the first of which is the general baccalauréat usually taken by pupils in general lycées; the second, baccalauréat technologique (technological baccalauréat), is offered to pupils in technical lycées and the third, baccalauréat professional, is vocational.

Bachelor of Education (BEd) This *degree* is awarded to students who qualify as teachers after a three or four year course of training. Courses are taught in departments of education in universities or in colleges of higher education and must meet requirements laid down by the *Department for Education* (DFE). The requirements differ according to age phases, i.e. *primary* and *secondary*. Secondary courses offer academic study and study of subject application for teaching; primary courses offer academic study and a range of *curriculum* courses. Training in both phases also includes teaching and education studies to complement familiarising experience of, and practice in, schools. Circulars 9/92 and 14/93 from the DFE have given impetus to new forms of school-based training in which schools and institutions of higher education are required to work as partners.

Applicants for BEd courses (now BA (*QTS*) courses in some institutions) must have passed *GCSE* or equivalent in Mathematics and English at the required levels (Grade C or above in GCSE). Applicants born on or after 1 September 1979 who enter primary courses after 1 September 1998 will also be expected to have attained a standard equivalent to GCSE Grade C or above in a science subject or in combined science. The science requirement will not apply to applicants for secondary courses. See *teacher training; university department of education (UDE)*.

backwardness Backwardness in pupils can be identified by their failure to *attain* to the same extent as most in the same *chronological age* group. The failure is not attributable to lack of *intelligence*; teachers

13

and *educational psychologists* believe that the causes may be traced to social or *emotional difficulties* and not to retardation. Retardation is often irredeemable because of lack of intelligence but many believe that backwardness is remediable. See *dyslexia; late developers; learning difficulty.*

Baker days   See *closure days.*

banding   This is a system adopted, in the main, by secondary schools for organising broad groups in a year group for teaching purposes. The criterion for banding is usually general *ability*; thus, a year group may be divided into two or more bands from which teaching groups are derived. The *timetable* often dictates that pupils have to be taught within the same band for nearly all subjects. See *class; mixed-ability; group; setting; streaming.*

Basic English   In the late 1920s C.K. Ogden devised a basic language of 850 words for effective, though limited, communication and, in time, it found a niche in the teaching of English to foreigners. See *English as a foreign language (EFL).*

basic skills   These *skills* are the minimum needed for meaningful participation in everyday life. In our society, the skills are derived from reading, writing and arithmetic – e.g. reading instructions, adding numbers – because we believe that meaningful participation is dependent on appropriate levels of *literacy* and *numeracy.* See *oracy; spelling; Standard English.*

behaviour   The *headteacher* is responsible for *discipline* but must take *governors'* views into account when formulating policy and taking action. The headteacher, too, must take responsibility for the decision to exclude a pupil; if the pupil is under 16, parents must be given the reasons for the *exclusion.* When a pupil is excluded for more than five days in any one term or is likely to forgo an opportunity to enter public examinations, the governors and the *LEA* must be informed.

Parents are entitled to take up the matter with governors and LEA. Both governors and LEA have a right to instruct the headteacher to reinstate pupils. There is a right of formal appeal for pupils who are permanently excluded; arrangements for this must be made by the LEA (or by governors in *voluntary-aided schools*), when they are required.

There is a different procedure in *self-governing schools*. Appeals are first made to the local Discipline Committee, a sub-group of the governing body. Further appeals against permanent exclusions may be made to the Appeal Committee, an independent group. The decision of this committee is binding. The decision of a Discipline Committee to uphold permanent exclusion must be reported to the LEA of the area as soon as possible. See *corporal punishment; detention; disruptive units; moral education; pastoral care; punishments.*

behavioural objective A behavioural objective is a predictive statement made by a teacher about the intended outcome of a lesson or series of lessons. The objective is focused on measurable aspects of changes in the learner's behaviour. It is widely used as a planning device but does not have universal appeal. Critics believe that it has a narrowing effect because the teacher may be tempted to set *objectives* for those aspects of learning which lend themselves to the approach. See *planned behaviour modification programme.*

behavioural problems Children are said to have behavioural problems when their behaviour patterns set them apart from the normal range of behaviours of their contemporaries. Such unusual behaviour, sometimes including disruption, verbal and physical intimidation, *bullying* and various other kinds of anti-social behaviour, can cause immense problems for teachers. Schools have their own rules and codes of behaviour to try to develop good behaviour and these may well include a policy on bullying. There may be an attempt to modify the behaviour of certain children through a *planned behaviour modification programme*. In extreme cases children with behavioural problems may be excluded from school. *Educational psychologists* would normally be asked to make an assessment of children with severe behaviour problems. See *backwardness; child guidance; disruptive units; emotional and behavioural difficulties (EBD); family therapy; hyperactivity; under achievement.*

behaviourism This is one of the major schools of psychology and is based on the premise that psychology is chiefly concerned with behaviour. It offers a theory and particular approach to psychological enquiry and relies on clearly defined objectivity in the collection of data. Its applications to schools are associated with the work of B.F. *Skinner*, both in a general theory of education and in the development of *programmed learning*. A principle of behaviourism is the positive reinforcement of desired behaviour; thus teachers praise intended learned behaviour and try to extinguish undesirable behaviour. For some critics such an approach is too deterministic and manipulative, giving a view of teaching as mainly about control. Nonetheless, the widespread use of systems of rewards and punishments in schools, including merit points, badges and house points, may be seen as the application of behaviourist principles in practice. See *planned behaviour modification programme*.

bilateral school   Under the *tripartite system* of secondary provision established under the 1944 Education Act, a bilateral school was based on two of three elements, namely grammar, technical or *secondary modern*. Pupils were taught in the same school but, depending on 11+ (eleven-plus) results or other test results, had to follow courses based on one element only, thus creating two distinct groups on the same site.

bilingual assistants   These are additional staff, usually part-time, provided by the *LEA* or school to support pupils and parents whose first language is not English. See *English as a foreign language (EFL)*; *language deficit; language support teachers; partnership teaching; Section II staff; support teachers*.

bilingual pupils   These are pupils who are known to speak more than one language in their daily lives. The term puts their language competences in a positive light. See *ethnic minority; partnership teaching*.

binary system   This system evolved during the expansion of the *higher education* sector in the 1960s. Polytechnics were established and coexisted with existing universities but were not equally regarded; in practice, therefore, a binary system emerged and was subsequently commended in the White Paper 'Education: A Framework for Expansion' (1972) as the basis for growth. Under the *Further and Higher Education Act (1992)*, polytechnics were redefined and given university status. See *Council for National Academic Awards (CNAA)*.

bipartite system   The system was made up of *selective* and *non-selective schools; technical schools* were not normally included, so pupils were selected for *grammar* or *secondary modern schools*. See *tripartite system*.

Black Papers   The Papers, first published in 1969 and continued into the 1970s, were polemical, attacked so-called progressive trends in education and called for the return or retention of traditional practices. The trends attacked included *child-centred approaches*, *discovery* methods of *learning* and *comprehensive schools*; practices to be retained included *selection* for secondary schooling and *streaming*, traditional teaching methods and the sponsorship of exclusive schools for able pupils who had special talents. Many of the ideas promoted through the Papers are now championed by groups such as the National Council for Educational Standards (NCES), the *Centre for Policy Studies* (CPS) and the *Hillgate Group*. Those who contributed to the Black Papers included Cyril Burt, A.E. Dyson, C.B. Cox and Kingsley Amis.

block practice   Student teachers undertake block *teaching practice* during training. It is termed block practice because it is continuous and occupies the whole of the time for a specified number of weeks when the student is required to be in school. Under serial practice arrangements, the student may be in school for an agreed number of days per week during a given period.

block release   Block release for agreed periods may be granted to employees in order to follow *vocational* courses at local colleges of further education. Employers have a vested interest in ensuring that workers gain appropriate qualifications. See *day release*.

block timetable   This is a timetable constructed to ensure that teaching and learning can benefit from the continuity of a long period – e.g. half a day – as opposed to short, single periods of 45–60 minutes.

Board of Education   The Board, a government department set up in 1900, was given powers to regulate the provision of suitable schools by local education authorities. The Board was formally ended in 1945 when the *Ministry of Education* came into being; the Ministry became the Department of Education and Science in 1964 and in 1992 the name was changed to the *Department for Education* (DFE). See *Butler Act (1944 Education Act)*.

boarding school   Pupils who attend boarding school are resident during terms, although some may go home at weekends. On the whole, these schools are in the *independent* sector; the small number found in the *state* sector are invariably for pupils with *special educational needs*. It has been estimated that less than two per cent of the school population are boarders. See *preparatory schools*; *Service Children's Education Authority*; *state boarding schools*.

borderline   Borderline refers to the agreed area of immediate marks above or below the *pass mark*. For example, if the pass mark is 40, then the agreed borderline boundaries could be set at 37 and 43. Examiners and examination boards normally scrutinise borderline cases with great care in order to ensure fairness. See *cut-off point*.

breadth   A term often used in descriptions or discussions of *curriculum*. It implies a range and balance of subject and *cross-curricular* elements as an important dimension in children's education. See *integrated course; interdisciplinary; liberal studies; whole curriculum*.

British Association for the Advancement of Science (BAAS)
BAAS, also known as the British Association, was founded in 1831 by scientists who were keen to maximise the contribution and importance of science and technology in society. The Association has 17 different sections, arranges annual conferences and endeavours to inform the public of advances in scientific areas. For further information contact:

British Association for the Advancement of Science
23 Savile Row
London
W1X 1AB

Telephone No: 0171 973 3500

British Council   The Council aims to foster cultural links and to disseminate knowledge of Britain. It is funded, in the main, by the Commonwealth Office and the Foreign Office and it promotes many educational activities in developing countries. For further information contact:

British Council
10 Spring Gardens
London
SW1A 2BN

Telephone No: 0171 930 8466

British Education Index (BEI)   The BEI is an important quarterly for academics and professionals in education. It lists and categorises the subject matter of articles published in this country and notes sources.

British and Foreign School Society   The Society grew from the endeavours of supporters of Joseph Lancaster who pioneered a system of primary schooling for poor children in the early nineteenth century. Originally founded as the Lancastrian Society, the name was changed by 1814 and its schools were renamed British Schools. The Society was seen as a force for social and educational improvement, was supported by influential people (e.g. James Hill and Lord Byron) and became active in other countries.

British Standard BS 5750   BS 5750 sets criteria for identifying *quality* systems. Some educational institutions aspire to these high *standards* and, if successful, may receive the award.

Bryce Commission   The Commission was set up in 1894 'to consider what are the best methods of establishing a well organised system of secondary education in England'. Under James Bryce, the Commission made important recommendations; secondary education, it was argued, should be under the central control of a Minister for Education but, at local level, should be the responsibility of local authorities. In addition, the need for *scholarships* for elementary pupils and a limited number of places for girls in the existing system were acknowledged.

budget   Under the goverment's arrangements for *local management of schools*, individual schools are given control over their own budgets and are expected to manage them in a business-like way. All secondary schools and large primary schools have exercised control since the end of 1993; small primaries and certain inner London schools followed suit in 1994.

Schools' budgets are calculated according to a *formula* devised by *LEAs*. The formula is devised to take account of such things as numbers of pupils in schools, local conditions and *capitation* levels under the previous system of funding.

Under Education (School Government) Regulations 1989 (SI 1989/1503) and Section 36 of the 1988 Act, budgetary control is delegated to governing bodies and, in practice, bodies tend to delegate control to sub-groups or to *headteachers*. *Governors* have a duty to ensure that accurate accounts of expenditure are kept (Section 39 (12) of the 1988 Act). Schools' spending can be monitored and governing bodies advised by the LEAs who, in cases of financial breakdown, can assume direct control over budgets (Section 37 of the 1988 Act).

Grant maintained schools are entitled to funding at the level which the former LEAs would have afforded, plus shares of the LEAs' central budgets. These shares are calculated by the *DFE* as percentage additions and are based on actual spending plans for LEAs in the previous year. Grant maintained schools receive their grants directly from the DFE. Equivalent funding is recouped from schools' former LEAs. See *Annual Maintenance Grant (AMG); Audit Commission; bursar; delegated budget; efficiency (of school); Funding Agency for Schools (FAS); General Schools Budget (GSB); standard spending assessment (SSA); zero budgeting approach.*

Bullock Report   In 1972, a Committee of Inquiry under Sir Alan Bullock was set up to examine all aspects of schools' approaches to the teaching of English. The Committee considered the processes of writing, reading and speaking; it examined ways to improve current practice and explored how procedures for monitoring levels of attainment in core skills might be used. The Report, entitled 'A Language for Life', was published in 1975; it recommended that schools should expand resources for teaching English and called for more in-service provision for teachers. Its major recommendations, however, focused on teachers and curriculum policy; every teacher, it claimed, needed to be a teacher of English and every school, from nursery to secondary, needed a language across the curriculum policy.

bullying   This subject is given widespread publicity and is a matter of great public concern. According to the Elton Report (1989), it tended to be 'ignored by teachers'; in recent years, many schools have implemented policies to counteract bullying and to ensure that victims are supported. Patterns of bullying may vary from school to school but it is said that boys rather than girls may be singled out as victims – usually in places outside the classroom. See *behaviour; behavioural problems.*

bursar   The bursar is the treasurer of a school or college but nowadays his or her responsibilities often extend beyond financial matters. Since the advent of *local management of schools* (LMS), the bursar's role has been enhanced; tasks may require participation in strategic planning, overseeing maintenance of buildings and handling public relations. See *budget; efficiency (of school); school secretary; zero budgeting approach.*

bursary   A bursary is an award in the form of a *grant* or remission of fees. It may be offered by fee-paying schools or awarding bodies in order to defray the cost of courses. See *articled teacher.*

bursary scheme   This scheme is intended to boost teacher-recruitment in *shortage subjects*, i.e. mathematics, physics, chemistry, *technology*. Students following initial *teacher training* courses in these subjects are awarded an extra amount per year at the current rate.

business education   The implementation of the *National Curriculum* gave further impetus to teaching and learning in this area. It was recommended that *economic and industrial understanding* should be made more explicit to all pupils in compulsory schooling. In addition, the content of business education courses has been substantially revised in order to reflect changes in *information technology* and business practice and to broaden the base of economic understanding.

Many institutions of higher education offer business studies degrees, a number of which focus on particular areas of world trade. Business qualifications are also offered by other organisations such as *Business and Technology Education Council* (BTEC) and *City and Guilds of London Institute* (CGLI). See *Compact*; *industry*; *work experience*.

Business and Technology Education Council (BTEC)   The Council was established in 1974 by the *Secretary of State* for Education under the name of Business and Technician Education Council. The name was changed in 1991 to Business and Technology Education Council in order to reflect an expanding range of interests.

The Council is involved in developing and appraising courses (in England and Wales) which have strong work-related, vocational components. These courses lead to BTEC qualifications in a growing number of areas – e.g. agriculture, business, caring, engineering, catering – and are alternative routes to higher education (HE) or employment. Sixth formers or school-leavers may enter the programme at First level; technicians and those of similar grade are likely to enter at the next level – National; finally, technicians and management trainees may be taught at the higher level – Higher National.

The general equivalences of BTEC qualifications are as follows:

- BTEC First Certificate = a minimum of 4 passes at GCSE level;
- BTEC National = A levels, qualification for entry to university in related courses;
- BTEC Higher National = close to pass degree standard.

BTEC courses are usually offered within modular schemes; there are core, compulsory modules and options and students can aim for Certificate or Diploma A level qualifications. The nature of the modules demands a variety of teaching and learning approaches – e.g. projects, work experience. Many employers approve the practical or hands on approaches and many students feel committed to study that is not wholly academic.

There is now much interest in aligning BTEC qualifications with others (e.g. *NVQ*) in this area. See *business education; Certificate of Pre-Vocational Education (CPVE); Ordinary National Certificate (ONC); Ordinary National Diploma.* For further information contact:

BTEC
Central House
Upper Woburn Place
London
WC1 0HH

Telephone No: 0171 413 8400

Butler Act (1944 Education Act)   The Act, named after R.A. Butler, President of the *Board of Education*, an astute thinker, was part of the blueprint for post-war reconstruction. The Act heralded important changes. The Board of Education was replaced by a *Ministry of Education* under a minister with increased powers to insist that *local education authorities* discharged their duties. The system of public schooling was arranged in three stages – *primary, secondary* and *further*. Within each stage, pupils were to be educated in accordance with age, ability and aptitude. The school-leaving age, then 14 years, was to be raised to 15 and then to 16 as soon as circumstances allowed. The principle of allowing the coexistence of *church* and *state schools* (*dual system*) was not affected but religious worship in all of them was made compulsory.

The Butler Act was a landmark; it established a triangular balancing of powers in which government was responsible for broad provision, local education authorities were responsible for local administration and services and teachers were responsible for curriculum and teaching. The framework lasted until 1988 when the *Education Reform Act* (ERA) redistributed responsibilities and powers.

~ C ~

Campaign for the Advancement of State Education (CASE)
CASE was founded in 1960 and is now an influential *pressure group*
made up of parents, teachers and others interested in education. The
Campaign is guided by an agreed, national policy and is built on the
support and activities of local groups. See *Home and School Council.*
For further information contact:

CASE
4 Hill Road
Carshalton
Surrey
SM5 3RJ

Telephone No: 0181 669 5929

capitation   Capitation is the annual sum passed on to the school by
the *local education authority* in order to pay running costs and buy con-
sumables and non-consumables. The amount passed on is dependent
on the total number of pupils on roll and the breakdown of their ages;
age is an important factor because older pupils are 'worth' more than
younger pupils. For example, Year 12 pupils attract more generous
funding than Year 7 pupils and secondary pupils attract more than
primary. Under the government's scheme, *local management of schools*
(LMS), nearly all local authority schools now have control over their
budgets. Capitation, therefore, is central to the amount calculated
under *formula funding*, i.e. funding of schools by a formula devised by
the local authority to comply with government's requirements. See
falling rolls.

careers education and guidance   A structured course and/or a
co-ordinated series of activities relating to pupils' futures. Particular
attention is given to choices and decisions likely to affect future education, training, employment and their lives as adults. See *counselling.*

catchment area   This is the area from which a school usually draws its pupils. Following the 1980 Education Act, parents were entitled to express preferences for places in local schools or in schools in other local authorities. Under the 1988 Education Act, schools with places available had to accede to parents' wishes although the updated *Parent's Charter* (1994) made clear that *selective* and *church schools* need not comply in certain circumstances. *Local education authorities* must follow detailed guidance from the government in managing school places and schools in their *prospectuses* must set out their own rules for allocating their own places. See *neighbourhood school.*

Centre for Educational Research and Innovation (CERI)
CERI operates under the aegis of the Organisation for Economic Cooperation and Development (OECD). In practice, it is an international agency for promoting and fostering research, reviewing and reporting on innovations and providing a centre through which member states can orchestrate their programmes and disseminate findings. For further information contact:

> Director for Education, Employment, Labour and Social Affairs
> OECD
> Château de la Muette
> 2 rue André Pascal
> Paris 16e
> France
>
> Telephone No: 00 33 1 45 24 82 00

Centre for Policy Studies (CPS)   The CPS is an influential think-tank of the Conservative new right. Its publications in the 1980s anticipated and helped to shape the government's educational reform programme. See *Black Papers.* For further information contact:

> Centre for Policy Studies
> 52 Rochester Row
> London
> SW1P 1JU
>
> Telephone No: 0171 828 1176

Certificate of Pre-Vocational Education (CPVE)   CPVE was announced as a new qualification by the Department of Education and Science (DES) in 1982 and was described in detail in '17 Plus – A

New Qualification'. It was implemented in 1983 when courses designed as a preparation for work were offered to students of 16+. The courses were coordinated by a board drawn from the *Business and Technology Education Council* (BTEC), *City and Guilds* (CGLI) and the *Royal Society of Arts* (RSA). CPVE was overtaken by changes in the 16–19 provision i.e. *National Vocational Qualifications* (NVQ). See *Diploma of Vocational Education (DVE)*.

Certificate of Secondary Education (CSE)   CSE was intended for school-leavers for whom GCE *O level* was too demanding. Both examinations were phased out in 1988 when the *General Certificate of Secondary Education* (GCSE), a unified examination for most 16-year-olds, was introduced.

Certificate of Sixth Year Studies (CSYS)   The Certificate is a Scottish qualification for *secondary* pupils. The pupils sit for higher grades at the end of their fifth year and continue studies into the sixth year.

chancellor   A chancellor is the head of a *university*, usually a nominal post. The post may be filled by a public figure who dignifies all the university's formal cermonies, e.g. conferment of *degrees*.

change of character   A change of character to a school may occur when a proposal to alter it in some fundamental way is made. Thus, selection by ability or reducing or extending the age range are changes likely to bring about a change of character and, as with all changes of this kind, would have to be approved by the *Secretary of State*.

charitable status   Groups seeking charitable status have to apply to, and be approved by, the *Charity Commission*. Approval is based on rules, some of which apply to suitability of a group's aim. Among the generally accepted aims are the support, improvement or advancement of education and it is aims such as these that allow parent–teacher and other groups to seek charitable status. Groups seeking or holding charitable status are subject to the provisions of the Charities Act (1992); the Act deals with aspects of status and regulates investment and oversight of funds. See *public schools*.

Charity Commission   In 1853, the Board of Charity Commissioners was established by the Charitable Trust Act to inquire into charities in England and Wales. The Commissioners were responsible for detecting and eradicating abuses (in some charities) and for initiating new schemes. For further information contact:

> Charity Commission
> St Albans House
> 57–60 Haymarket
> London
> SW17 4QX
>
> Telephone No: 0171 210 4477

Chief Education Officer (CEO) The Chief Education Officer, known as the Director of Education in some areas, is the head of the education service in a local authority and ensures that all statutory obligations are met. As head of the service, he/she reports directly to the *education committee* and oversees the implementation of its policies.

child abuse The term is now widely defined to include a wide range of sexual, emotional and physical abuses. Public awareness of the problem has been raised in recent years; accumulated evidence shows that abuse occurs in all strata of society and involves both boys and girls.

Social services departments maintain 'at risk' registers of the names of children who have been abused – or are likely to be abused. Teachers who suspect abuse of pupils are required to follow schools' internal arrangements for contacting the *Education Welfare Officer* (EWO) or other nominated persons from social services departments. See *child protection*. For further information contact:

> *Childline*
> The Royal Mail Building
> 50 Studd Street
> London
> N1 0QJ
>
> (Free counselling on 0800 1111)
>
> National Society for the Prevention of Cruelty to Children (NSPCC)
> 42 Curtain Road
> London
> EC2A 3NH
>
> Telephone No: 0171 825 2500

child care   See *pre-school education; pre-school playgroup*.

child-centred approach   This approach to education is guided by considerations of the child's needs as learner and not by the external requirements of teacher-imposed methods or curriculum. In essence, it seeks to exploit children's natural curiosity and interest and to engage them in active ways in their own learning. The approach has been influential in English primary education; it is praised by some as humane and criticised by others because, if taken to its logical conclusion, it lacks structure and coherence and is difficult to plan. See *Piaget, Jean; teaching method; teaching style*.

child guidance   This guidance is intended for identifying children's *emotional, behavioural* or developmental difficulties and for drawing up programmes of treatment. The resources for guidance are usually concentrated in clinics; *educational psychologists*, psychiatrists and social workers usually work as teams and, in many cases, adopt a *family therapy* approach. See *diagnostic assessment; school psychological service*.

child in need   The *Children Act (1989)* identifies a child in need as one who has disabilities and/or requires help to remain in satisfactory health. Children in need under the age of five are the responsibility of *social services* departments; children in need above that age are the responsibility of these departments outside school hours and school terms. In most cases, the responsibilities are shared with *local education authorities*.

child protection   It is generally accepted that parents give schools the power to act in loco parentis and that, in emergencies, schools should act independently to safeguard pupils or ensure prompt medical attention. Schools must also protect children in other respects; there must be a designated teacher and procedures for reporting suspected *child abuse* to *social services* departments, police and the NSPCC. Teachers should be trained for this role and be familiar with the work of *Area Child Protection Committees*.

Childline   This is a free telephone counselling service for children who believe that they are being abused. The lines are open 24 hours a day – 0800 1111. See *child abuse*. For further information contact:

Childline
The Royal Mail Building
50 Studd Street
London
N1 0QJ

childminders   Childminders are paid by parents/guardians of pre-school children to look after them during working hours on a daily or weekly basis. Minding is usually done in minders' homes and must comply with the requirements laid out in the *Children Act (1989)*. For further information contact:

The Day Care Trust
Wesley House
4 Wild Court
London
WC2P 5AU

Telephone No: 0171 405 5617

Children Act (1989)   The Act, consisting of ten parts and 14 schedules, was an important landmark in the history of child welfare. It came into force in 1991 and brought together a number of separate laws. The new coherence placed emphasis on the child's welfare in discussions and decisions on upbringing, acknowledged the family as the normal focus of this upbringing and gave much responsibility to *social services* departments for the smooth working of the Act.

The intention of the Act was to codify and strengthen the entitlement of children to certain rights in the areas of physical and mental protection, education and standards of care. For further information contact:

Child Poverty Action Group
4th Floor
1–5 Bath Street
London
EC1V 9PY

Telephone No: 0171 253 3406

choice of school   See *Parents' Charter*.

chronological age   Chronological age is calculated from the date of birth and is one of the organising principles of pupil groups or classes.

church schools   Church schools are influenced by particular religious beliefs which may permeate their atmospheres and values and characterise their approaches to education. A church school can be of two kinds, *independent* or *state*. If it is independent, it is likely to be controlled by a minority religious group – e.g. Quakers, Muslims – and is not funded by the state. If it is a state school it is funded through the *local education authority* but the level of funding depends on its status as *voluntary-controlled* or *voluntary-aided*. Voluntary-controlled schools are funded in full by the local education authority, follow the same RE syllabus as other schools in the authority and have church nominees on the board of governors. Voluntary-aided schools receive 85 per cent of funding from the state (through the local education authority) and are broadly guided in religious matters by trustees. See *dual system; spiritual, moral social and cultural development*.

circulars   These documents are prepared by the *Department for Education* as announcements or guidance on educational policies. Although signed by the *Secretary of State* or his/her nominee, circulars are not legally binding but *local education authorities* and further education and higher education institutions need to consider their implied and explicit expectations. See *law*.

citizenship   'Education for Citizenship', described in 'Curriculum Guidance Number 8', is one of the 'cross-curricular themes' relating to preparation for adult life in the *National Curriculum*. Preparation is based on eight 'essential elements': community; a plural society; citizen's rights and responsibilities; the family; democracy; citizen and the law; work, leisure and employment; the public services.

City and Guilds (CGLI)   The full name is the City and Guilds of London Institute and the abbreviated form usually refers to a range of *vocational*, work-related qualifications. See *business education; Certificate of Pre-Vocational Education (CPVE); Royal Society of Arts (RSA)*. For further information about qualifications contact:

City and Guilds of London Institute
76 Portland Place
London
W1N 4AA

Telephone No: 0171 278 2468

City Technology Colleges (CTCs)   The scheme for CTCs was launched by Kenneth Baker in 1986. He hoped that 20 colleges would be established by 1990 but, by May 1991, there were only 15.

The colleges are part of *secondary* (11–18) provision and, in the main, have a bias towards science and *technology*. The government and private sponsors (e.g. charities, businesses) jointly fund the ventures, all of which are outside *LEAs'* control. Initially, sponsors were expected to meet capital costs (buildings and equipment) and the government paid the running costs. Sponsors, in effect, are the owners of the colleges. Pupils are selected, fees are not charged and there is no legal requirement to follow the *National Curriculum*. The colleges have aroused some controversy. To date, they have failed to attract the level of sponsorship envisaged, are more generously funded (by government) than mainstream schools and, according to some educationalists, they are divisive.

There has been discussion about broadening the scheme by introducing new kinds of partnerships – e.g. with LEAs – and giving further consideration to ways in which maintained secondary schools might commit themselves to higher levels of achievement in technology, science and mathematics.

For further information, telephone: DFE Technology Colleges Unit – 0171 925 5838.

For specific information about sponsorship, telephone: The City Technology Colleges Trust – 0171 376 2511.

class   A class is a group of students organised for teaching purposes. In schools, pupils are normally grouped according to age although in some schools family grouping may be used. Grouping may also be organised according to ability. See *banding*; *form*; *mixed-ability group*; *mixed-age class*; *setting*; *streaming*.

class size   There is no national agreement on class size. *Headteachers* have to decide the size of classes in accordance with their resources and demands on school budgets but, under the 1988 Local Government Act, *governors* are ultimately responsible for the level of staffing. See *pupil–teacher ratio*.

classroom assistants   Classroom assistants are often known as *welfare assistants*. In *primary schools* they sometimes work with teachers in classrooms and may be employed for a specific task, e.g. helping a pupil with a disability. Outside classrooms, they may be employed to assist with library work or preparing materials or equipment. They usually work under the supervision of teachers. See *specialist teacher assistant* (STA).

Clause 28   Under Clause 28 of the 1988 Local Government Act, the promotion of homosexuality by local authorities is forbidden. The interpretation of the clause is often a cause for concern; school libraries, drama productions and other aspects of the school's provision and activities could come under scrutiny or be subjected to challenge. See *sex education*.

closure days   These are the five days each year when schools are closed to pupils, but staff attend to engage in *in-service education and training*. They were originally introduced by Kenneth Baker when he was Secretary of State for Education (1986–89), hence the alternative description of these days as Baker days. These days are part of a teacher's formal contractual duties and attendance at INSET organised on these five days is obligatory. The activities organised on closure days usually take place in schools. See *staff development*.

Cloze procedure   The procedure is designed to test the *readability* of texts by uncovering the levels of *reading* difficulty they present. Students are required to comprehend a passage from which a number of the words are omitted by supplying substitutes appropriate to the contexts.

code of practice (for special educational needs)   Under the Education Act 1993, the *Secretary of State* was directed to give practical guidance to all *maintained schools*, *local education authorities* and others engaged in identifying, assessing, providing for and monitoring pupils with *special educational needs*. The code took effect from autumn 1994.

co-education   Co-education is the education of both sexes in mixed classes in the same school. Most primary schools and a high proportion of secondary schools educate boys and girls together. It is claimed that girls' academic achievements are generally better in *single-sex schools*. See *sexism*.

cognitive development/growth   The term is often found in accounts of child and/or human development. Cognition refers more narrowly to the mental processes of knowing as the child grows and extends his or her powers to perceive ideas. See *concept*.

collaborative/cooperative groupwork   In some schools, groups of pupils may be arranged or evolve for certain learning activities. Teachers believe that pupils learn from each other and that the arrangement facilitates the development of social and interpersonal skills. *Groupwork* is common in primary schools but is also practised in secondary schools, especially in Years 7 and 8.

college of education   During the expansion of *teacher training* in the early 1960s, the number of colleges increased to 115. The *Robbins Report* (1963) recommended that the colleges should be known as colleges of education. By 1972, a reduction in the number of training places was unavoidable; 'Education: A Framework for Expansion' (White Paper) had predicted a surplus of teachers and, to rationalise the system, some colleges of education were absorbed into existing polytechnics or *universities* or were renamed institutes of *higher education*. As teacher training contracted, institutes were able to diversify and offer courses for qualifications in other areas.

College of Preceptors   The College aims to provide courses and qualifications for serving teachers and promotes professionalism. It received a Royal Charter in 1849 and, for some time afterwards, endeavoured to set itself up as a central council for registering qualified teachers. The endeavours were unsuccessful and, to date, no such council yet exists. See *General Teaching Council*. For further information contact:

> College of Preceptors
> Coppice Row
> Theydon Bois
> Epping
> Essex
> CM16 7DN
>
> Telephone No: 01992 812727

collegiate university   A collegiate university is based on a group of colleges each of which has much autonomy in organising its own affairs within the wider *university* regulations. Each college acts independently in admitting *undergraduates* and appointing staff. Oxford and Cambridge are the best-known collegiate universities.

combined course In *National Curriculum* terms, a combined course draws together two or more *short courses* from non-foundation subjects/areas and/or *foundation subjects*.

Committee of Vice-Chancellors and Principals (CVCP) Membership of CVCP is afforded to heads of *universities*. The Committee is a representative, standing group which promotes the interests of universities and makes known its views to government and funding councils. For further information contact:

CVCP
29 Tavistock Square
London
WC1H 9EZ

Telephone No: 0171 387 9231

common curriculum 'Common' may imply that it is a *curriculum* for all pupils in all schools or for all pupils in the same school. Both ideas rest on the assumption that all pupils will have common teaching–learning experiences which are ultimately related to beliefs in common culture.

Common Entrance Examination This examination is usually taken by 12- or 13-year-olds who wish to gain places in *independent* (especially *public*) *schools*. The examination is devised by groups from a girls' schools board and boys' common entrance committee but candidates' answers may be marked by the schools of their choice. It has been estimated that 10,000 boys and 4,000 girls sit the examination each year. See *preparatory schools*.

community education The philosophy of community education is strongly related to beliefs in education as a lifelong or continuing process. The process is continued in and through *community schools and colleges* and may be extended beyond their physical boundaries by teachers who go out to teach classes in other locations, e.g. parish halls, local centres. See *adult education; continuing education; evening classes; extra-mural studies*.

community schools and colleges The community ideal encourages a wide involvement of local people of all ages in education and learning. Schools and colleges in many areas, therefore, organise educational activities in which adults may participate alongside older, secondary pupils during the day and/or make use of the same facilities for classes in the evening. As schools assume responsibility for their own budgets, it is likely that educational activities will be extended as *headteachers* endeavour to increase income by maximising the use of schools' facilities. See *adult education; continuing education; evening classes; extra-mural studies*.

community service In many secondary schools, pupils are encouraged to work voluntarily as part of a national programme, e.g. *Duke of Edinburgh Award*, or as part of a school's contribution to the local community. The pupils might be asked to help in primary schools, old people's homes or day centres. Community service is favoured sometimes by magistrates and others as an appropriate alternative to fines or periods in custody for young offenders.

Community Service Volunteers (CSV) CSV is funded by the *Department for Education* (DFE), private bodies and local authorities. The service was established in 1962 to assist youth workers with communal activities in which young people participate. For further information contact:

CSV
237 Pentonville Road
London
N1 9NJ

Telephone No: 0171 278 6601

Compact Compact is a scheme designed to boost pupils' achievement through forging links between particular schools and local business and *industry*. It was started in London and received favourable comments in reports on schools in the scheme by *HMIs*. The scheme guarantees that effort and achievement will be recognised by employers. They agree to give priority in interviews and offers of employment to pupils who achieve specified levels of attendance and punctuality, complete coursework and community projects and successfully undertake a period of *work experience*.

comparability Comparability is the process through which levels of achievement in *coursework* or *examinations* for different courses leading to the same award can be judged.

compensation   Compensation in *assessment* may only be considered when regulations allow. It is a device through which low *attainment* in *coursework* or poor *examination* result (in one paper) in a particular area of a prescribed *syllabus* can be compensated for by high attainment or very good examination results in other areas.

compensatory education   This approach to education is intended to redress a perceived deficit in learning; for example, children from *ethnic minority* groups are sometimes perceived in this way and were taught under special arrangements in order to overcome their cultural deficits. See *deficit model; disadvantaged; Head Start; language deficit; positive discrimination; special educational needs* (SEN); *underachievement.*

competence   Competence can be understood as a capacity or capability in the learner or as an element of occupational role. 'Capacity' or 'capability' and 'element' may be inseparable in some instances but the distinction remains and the term may be defined differently according to context. In post-compulsory education and training, for example, there is a strong leaning towards occupational competence assessed by outcomes. In teacher education, the government has imposed competency-based models for primary and secondary training; the long-term aim is to improve the quality of teaching by concentrating on classroom skills.

competitive tendering   Under competitive tendering arrangements, private organisations may compete by tendering for certain services – e.g. school meals, cleaning – previously the preserve of the *local education authority*. Tendering is now an established part of the market approach and is intended to ensure good value for money.

complaints   See *ombudsman.*

comprehensive school   The comprehensive school was officially defined as 'one which is intended to cater for the secondary education of all children in a given area' (Circular 144/1947). Following the perceived failings of the *tripartite system*, comprehensive schools were introduced and their number increased in the 1960s and 1970s. The Education Act of 1976 sought to confirm the comprehensive as the only kind of *state secondary school* but was repealed three years later. Existing comprehensive schools cater for the vast majority of pupils in England, Wales and Scotland but not in Northern Ireland where there is *selection*. There is no uniform pattern and, in practice, 'comprehensive' is interpreted in different ways; for example, some schools have retained their former names – e.g. 'grammar' or 'high' – and there are no agreed, common principles for organising pupil groups, so *streaming, setting* or *mixed ability* are used in line with schools' differing aims. See *grammar schools; multilateral education; non-selective schools; secondary modern school; single-sex* school.

concept   Much has been written about the formation and nature of the concept. In essence, the learner must first be able to generalise. Generalising requires abilities to perceive common elements or patterns in objects, behaviours and situations and to raise understanding of them to a level of abstraction. In order to do this, the learner must be able to discriminate between what is relevant and irrelevant to a particular concept. To a large extent, therefore, concept formation is dependent on powers of discrimination and classification which, if exercised successfully, help to establish a cognitive system through which data are interpreted.

contact ratio   Teachers' *timetables* consist of contact time, i.e. when they are teaching, and *non-contact time*, when they prepare lessons, mark pupils' work or perform administrative tasks. Contact ratio, therefore, refers to the average number of hours of actual teaching in one week or two, depending on particular schools' preferences. The ratio is usually expressed as a decimal fraction or as a percentage of the total hours in the weekly or fortnightly timetable. See *free periods; teacher–class ratio*.

continuing education   The philosophy underlying continuing education is that real learning is a lifelong process and embraces a wide range of experiences – not merely formal learning in schools, colleges and *universities*. See *adult education; community education; community schools and colleges; distance learning; educational television; evening class; extra-mural studies; mature students; National Institute of Adult Continuing Education (NIACE); open admission; Open College of the Arts; open learning; Open University; University of the Third Age (U3A); Workers' Education Association (WEA)*.

continuity and progression   The two terms are now almost inextricable. Continuity is now widely used in *National Curriculum* contexts to refer to the planning and order of arrangements for teaching, learning and other experiential activities as a framework for pupils' development. *Progression* is an essential part of this framework; teachers must take pupils' previous learning into account and build on it with appropriate sequencing of further learning activities. See *programmed learning*.

continuous assessment This approach requires the *assessment* of students' work throughout a course or given period and it may be adopted instead of, or in conjunction with, a formal *examination*. Continuous assessment, it is claimed, requires consistent effort from students throughout a course and is beneficial to those who suffer from examination nerves. Since it allows *feedback* on assignments completed, assessment is *formative* so students are aware of their levels of performance. It is also suggested, however, that, at school level, the increase in *coursework* may discriminate against pupils whose home circumstances for studying are difficult. See *homework*.

convergent thinking In this approach to *problem-solving*, thinking is focused on finding a single solution which, by implication, is the one right answer. Learners who adopt this approach are usually known as 'convergers'.

coordinator The coordinator is the teacher who takes the lead in promoting and coordinating teaching and learning in a particular subject or *curriculum* area. In *primary schools*, coordinators may also be needed to oversee *key stages*.

core subjects English, mathematics and science are considered more important than others in the *National Curriculum* and are known as core subjects. These subjects must be taught to all pupils during the years of compulsory schooling. See *foundation subject*; *options*.

corporal punishment The physical beating of pupils was abolished in *state schools* – and for pupils in *independent schools* whose fees are wholly or partly paid from public funds – in 1987. However, corporal punishment may still be used for private fee-paying students in independent schools, provided there are more than 50 boarders. See *behaviour*; *discipline*; *punishments*; *Society of Teachers Opposed to Physical Punishment (STOPP)*.

correlation Correlation is the measure or extent to which two or more different collections of data, obtained from the same sample, are related. The measure is shown as a coefficient, i.e. the correlation coefficient on a scale of +1.00 to –1.0; 0.0 indicates no correlation, +1.0 is perfect and –1.0 is complete inversion.

correspondence course See *distance learning*.

correspondence theory Correspondence theorists often claim that the purpose of schooling is to satisfy the needs of an industrial world. Schools, they argue, anticipate these needs by training pupils to be deferential, compliant, punctual and industrious so that they (pupils) will be prepared for their future occupations as assembly line workers, checkers, clerks and similar jobs based on routines. See *industry*.

Council for Education in World Citizenship (CEWC) CEWC, founded in 1939, is a non-political organisation concerned with global issues, e.g. world health. It sustains a programme of conferences and seminars for older pupils and teachers and has a centre in London. For further information contact:

> Council for Education in World Citizenship
> Seymour Mews House
> Seymour Mews
> London
> W1H 9PE
>
> Telephone No: 0171 935 1752

Council of Local Education Authorities (CLEA) CLEA was formed by the merger of the *Association of County Councils* (ACC) and the *Association of Metropolitan Authorities* (AMA) in 1975. The Council (CLEA) speaks for the Authorities on matters affecting their responsibilities and duties and makes known their views to the *Secretary of State*. For further information contact:

> Council of Local Education Authorities
> Eaton House
> 66A Eaton Square
> Westminster
> London
> SW1W 9BH
>
> Telephone No: 0171 235 1200/9554

Council for National Academic Awards (CNAA) The CNAA was established in 1964 as the *degree*-awarding body for the non-university *higher education* sector, i.e. the colleges and polytechnics. It became a formidable power for change and development in higher education, especially in the areas of course design and assessment. The Council was abolished in 1992 when the *binary* line was removed, establishing the polytechnics as new *universities* and enabling them to confer their own degrees.

counselling   In the broad sense, counselling is intended to foster self-examination of motives and behaviour so that people can be helped to make up their own minds. The conclusions they draw need to be consistent with their decisions and resources for re-defining and sustaining relationships or focusing on future moves. In the narrow sense, counselling of pupils in schools is usually concerned with personal issues, educational progress and vocational intentions. See *careers education and guidance; guidance; pastoral care; personal and social education (PSE); spiritual, moral, social and cultural development.*

coursework   Coursework consists of assignments such as essays, *projects*, reports, paintings and so on completed by pupils during a course, e.g. *GCSE*. The assignments are undertaken during lessons or as *homework* and are normally *assessed* according to criteria. Marks or *grades* attained for assignments are taken into account when the overall result is calculated at the end of the course. See *continuous assessment.*

craft, design and technology (CDT)   CDT grew from what used to be known as metalwork in secondary schools but now encompasses a wider range of materials and ideas which include problem-solving, design and computer-work. It is included in the *National Curriculum* as part of the design and technology component. See *information technology (IT); National Association for Education in Art and Design.*

crammer   The term used to describe institutions which specialise in preparing students for specific public examinations. Normally independent, fee-paying colleges, the slightly pejorative term 'crammer' alludes to the supposed process of cramming information into the brain for the short-term goal of passing an examination. In fact, some crammers provide good, intensive courses of instruction which are based on well-developed instructional techniques. See *private tuition.*

credit   In some universities and colleges of higher education, students progress to final awards by accumulating credit points for successful completion of modules or courses. In some instances, credits may be transferred with a student from one institution to another. See *accreditation.*

Credit Accumulation and Transfer Scheme (CATS) The Transfer Scheme facilitates the transfer of a student's credit from one institution to another. It is based on an agreed number of credits for different stages in undergraduate or masters programmes (part-time or full-time). See *accreditation*. In undergraduate programmes the stages are normally as follows:

- 120 credits – certificate;

- 240 credits – diploma;

- 360 credits – degree.

criterion-referenced test This kind of *test* is used to calibrate a student's performance against a pre-determined *standard*. The performance is not measured against the performances of others but is scored or assessed by reference to known criteria. See *grades; impression making; norm-referenced testing.*

cross-curricular A subject-based *curriculum* emphasises the compartmentalisation of subjects and strong boundaries between them; cross-curricular approaches are based on finding links and similarities in the contents of different subjects and in relating them to show curriculum knowledge in a differing light. The *National Curriculum* definition suggests that cross-curricular notions are embedded in themes (e.g. industrial or business understanding) and dimensions (e.g. equal opportunities and skills) all of which contribute to the *whole curriculum*. Curriculum and *timetable* planners have to bear cross-curricular elements in mind. See *advisory teacher; breadth; integrated course; interdisciplinary.*

curriculum The term may be defined in different ways. The broad definition embraces all intended and unintended *learning* in school, college or university; the narrow view is one in which curriculum is perceived as a predetermined, narrow range of instructional activities. See *common curriculum; hidden curriculum; integrated work; interdisciplinary; National Curriculum; options; syllabus; whole curriculum.*

Curriculum and Assessment Authority for Wales (ACAC) The Authority was known as the Curriculum Council for Wales (CCW) until 1993 when the name was changed. ACAC is an advisory body to the *Secretary of State* for Wales on all aspects of the *National Curriculum*. See *Welsh Office Education Department (WOED)*. For further information contact:

Curriculum and Assessment Authority for Wales
Castle Buildings
Womanby Street
Cardiff
CF1 9SX

Telephone No: 01222 34494

curriculum guidelines   The guidelines were first drawn up by the *National Curriculum Council* (NCC), replaced by the *School Curriculum and Assessment Authority* (SCAA). They (guidelines) outline ways in which the teaching and learning of particular subjects or *curriculum* areas can be organised.

cut-off point   This is the point at which a *rank* order list, e.g. those used for marks or examination results, is agreed to separate passes from failures or decide boundaries between other classifications. Candidates whose marks fall within three or four per cent above or below the classification mark are *borderline* cases and are usually closely scrutinised by examiners and moderators. See *pass mark*.

day nurseries   These nurseries are normally provided by *social services* departments for children under the age of five. Since the number of places is limited, priority is usually given to children from disadvantaged backgrounds or to those who may be statemented for *special educational needs* (SEN) when they begin compulsory schooling. The nurseries are run by qualified staff and remain open throughout the day to meet the needs of working parents. See *nursery school; pre-school education*.

day release   Courses organised on a day release basis in *further* or *higher education* are intended to cater for employees who, by agreement with their employers, attend colleges for one or two days each week in order to study for approved qualifications. See *block release; in-service education and training*.

day school   The term implies that pupils are on the premises only during school hours; the pupils are not classified as boarders, whatever the status or description of the school.

dean   In an old-fashioned sense, a college or *university* dean is responsible for disciplining students. Nowadays, a dean may be a *head of department* or *faculty* in *further* or *higher education*.

Dearing, Sir Ron   In April 1993, the *Secretary of State* for Education, John Patten, asked Sir Ron, then chair designate of the *School Curriculum and Assessment Authority* (SCAA), to revise the framework for the *National Curriculum* (NC) and its assessment in order to make them manageable without loss of rigour. He consulted widely, prepared an interim report (July 1993) and put his final report to the Secretary of State at the end of the year.

deficit model   'Deficit' implies that the learner has a cultural deficiency that impedes learning in school. As a theoretical explanation for *underachievement* of working-class or *ethnic minority* groups, the model was influential in locating the reasons for failure in the home and background. Findings from research suggested that the explanation may be incomplete; underachievement could be an outcome of inadequate teaching and other factors in an ineffective school. See *compensatory education; disadvantaged; language deficit.*

degrees Students who successfully complete specified courses of study in *universities* and *higher education* institutions are awarded degrees. Awards are made in accordance with the level of study – Bachelor, Masters or Doctor.

At Bachelor level, students usually study for a period of three years; typical awards are Bachelor of Arts (BA), Bachelor of Education (BEd) and Bachelor of Science (BSc).

At Masters level, the award is a *higher degree* and the period of study may be up to two years after achieving a Bachelor's degree. *Graduates* of Oxford or Cambridge may apply to their universities for the degree and pay the appropriate fee after a required period of seven years (from *matriculation*).

A Doctorate – i.e. PhD or DPhil – is normally awarded following successful presentation of a *thesis*. Higher doctorates, for example Doctor of Literature (DLitt), may be awarded if books and other publications are submitted and deemed acceptable. See *diploma; graduate; honours degree; honorary degree; postgraduate studies; undergraduate.*

delegacy Delegacies are groups in universities empowered to undertake particular tasks and responsibilities. In Oxford, for example, there is a delegacy responsible for school examinations, overseeing the work of the Oxford examination board. A delegacy is commonly responsible to a higher committee in the university for the conduct of its work.

delegated budget A delegated budget is the whole or part budget allocated to school *governors* who must oversee its use at different stages. Budgets may also be delegated within institutions on a departmental or faculty basis. See *budget; efficiency (of school).*

department Secondary schools are usually organised on department or faculty lines. In the former, departments are based on subjects; in the latter, subjects are grouped as the basis for faculties. Departments and faculties are led by experienced teachers known as *Heads of Department* (HODs) or Heads of Faculties (HOFs). They are responsible to *headteachers* for nearly all aspects of their subject(s).

Department for Education (DFE)   In July 1992, the Department of Education and Science (DES) was officially replaced by the Department for Education. The change did not affect its global responsibilities for education. For further information contact:

> Department for Education
> Sanctuary Buildings
> Great Smith Street
> London
> SW1P 3BT

> Telephone No: 0171 925 5000.

Department of Education Northern Ireland (DENI)   Public education at all levels in Northern Ireland is managed by DENI. Five local controlling authorities were set up under the Education and Libraries (Northern Ireland) Order 1972. Boards acting for the authorities are required to sustain appropriate levels of resources in their areas. Integrated schools for Catholics and Protestants, established under the 1978 Education (Northern Ireland) Act and given further support by the Education Reform (Northern Ireland) Order (1990), function as the direct responsibility of the Northern Ireland Council for Integrated Education. For further information contact:

> Department of Education Northern Ireland
> Rathgael House
> Balloo Road
> Bangor
> County Down
> BT19 7PR

> Telephone No: 01247 270077

Department of Education and Science (DES)   See *Department for Education* (DFE).

Department of Trade and Industry (DTI)   The DTI is very interested in fostering links between education and *industry* as part of a long-term, national strategy. It has set up an industrial placement scheme for teachers and funded initiatives for introducing design and technology. For further information contact:

Department of Trade and Industry
Kingsgate House
68–74 Victoria Street
London
SW1E 6SW

Telephone No: 0171 215 2859

deputy head As a senior member of staff, this postholder is expected to deputise for the *headteacher*. In practice, he/she may be a mediator between the head and staff and must assume delegated responsibilities. The number of deputy heads in a school is usually determined by its size but, under *local management of schools*, the number of appointments at this level may be diminishing.

de-schooling In the 1970s, the belief that a purer education might be developed without the need for schools or schooling was promoted by Ivan Illich. He castigated the school's cumbersome bureaucracy, cost and ineffectiveness and urged developing countries to give serious consideration to his views on the relationship between schooling, economics and jobs. See *free school*.

Design and Technology (DT) See *craft, design and technology (CDT)*.

designated course These courses are listed by the *Department for Education* (DFE) and candidates offered places on them are given *mandatory awards*, subject to qualifying rules, by the *local education authority*. Students who gain places on unlisted courses can apply for *discretionary awards*.

detention This is a widespread and well-known sanction in schools. Pupils who break school rules or behave badly may be detained during morning break, lunchtime or immediately after normal school hours. In addition, offenders may have to complete assignments during detention. When children are detained after school it is important that the parents are informed of the exact circumstances of the detention before it takes place. See *discipline; punishments*.

development plan Schools, colleges and universities now produce plans to show progress to date, map developments, anticipate resource needs and decide how future progress will be identified and measured. See *school development plan*.

developmental testing Curriculum and associated materials can be subjected to developmental testing. The materials, in draft form, can be used by pupils or students who trial them – i.e. try them out. Feedback from the learners can then be used to modify the materials before the final versions are produced. See *evaluation; pilot study*.

diagnostic assessment Diagnostic assessment is undertaken to establish the range and depth of pupils' *learning difficulties*. The assessment may be made by an *educational psychologist* or suitably qualified teacher. When difficulties have been diagnosed, a programme of specific help can then be devised. See *screening; statement*.

dialect See *Standard English*.

differentiated examinations *Examinations* of this kind are designed for different *ability* levels; a number of different examination papers may have to be employed. In many examinations, there is a compulsory paper, parts of which may be easier or harder; the content and arrangement of parts may depend on the subject and the overall strategy for *testing* at different levels. See *matching*.

differentiation Learners differ in their needs, *aptitudes* and capabilities and differentiation is an acknowledgement of the differences. As far as learning and teaching are concerned, the term is best explained as the process of *matching* learning tasks to particular groups or individuals. Teachers, therefore, have to consider differences when planning and teaching lessons in order to ensure that all *abilities* in the class are catered for. The approach can be based on differentiation by task or by outcome.

difficulty index The index is often used in preparing and refining *tests* in order to determine the difficulty presented by individual items. It might simply indicate the percentage who respond incorrectly to certain items; items having high or low measures of difficulty may have to be withdrawn or replaced before the test is adopted.

diploma The diploma is an award made at the end of a course of specified length. Successful students may gain the qualification at a level below that of *degree* (or above, e.g. *PGCE*).

Diploma of Higher Education (DipHE) A DipHE course is equivalent to two years' study at first *degree* level. In practice, successful students normally proceed to a third year in order to gain degrees.

Many institutions now offer the DipHE within modular structures in which credit points can be accumulated and, if necessary, can be carried between participating colleges and universities. See *Credit Accumulation and Transfer Scheme*.

Diploma of Vocational Education (DVE) The DVE was intended for the 14 to 19 age group. It grew from the *Certificate of Pre-Vocational Education* (CPVE), a post-16 qualification. There are two levels (post-16), namely Intermediate (*GNVQ* level 2) and National (GNVQ level 3). Trials for DVE were conducted in 1991–2 and they were introduced soon afterwards. See *vocational education*.

direct grant school This type of school was introduced in 1926 to cater for selected intakes into the secondary age phase. The grant to support it was paid directly from government and the school had to ensure that a number of its places were always allocated to pupils from state primary schools (paid for by the local education authorities). Direct grant schools ceased to function after 1976; they chose to become *independent* or *maintained*.

direct method The direct method of teaching modern languages lays great emphasis on the teacher's oral approach; conversation, role play, questioning and answering are fostered at the expense of incremental grammar teaching – although grammar is not ignored but taught in context. See *teaching method*.

Director of Education See *Chief Education Officer*.

disadvantaged Disadvantaged learners are those whose learning is constrained by social factors, physical or mental disability or family circumstances. Some sociologists suggest that disadvantage may be endemic because of the nature of our society. See *compensatory education; deficit model; Head Start; language deficit; learning difficulty; underachievement*.

disapplication For certain specified reasons, *National Curriculum* requirements may be suspended for some pupils or groups identified by the *Education Secretary*. Disapplication is the process through which suspension may be effected. See *modifications; special educational needs (SEN)*.

discipline Discipline goes beyond narrow ideas of classroom control or teacher in charge. Many see it as a system of school rules through which rewards and *punishments* are used but, in a wider sense, the system is only one manifestation of a school's ethos and philosophy. The Education Act (1986) gave *headteachers* the responsibility for formulating and enforcing rules, within a framework of general principles provided by school *governors*. See *behaviour; corporal punishment; disruptive units; moral education.*

disciplines of education   These disciplines are psychology, history and philosophy of education and they used to be in vogue as major elements in teacher training. Sociology was added in the 1960s and tended to replace either history or philosophy – and sometimes both. In recent years, the disciplines have been displaced by greater emphasis on such things as practice, competence and relating theory to practice and vice versa.

discovery learning   See *child-centred approach.*

discretionary award   *Local education authorities* have discretion in making certain awards. Such awards have to be made in accordance with authorities' own guidelines. The awards are normally made for sub-first degree courses. See *grants.*

disruptive units   Disruptive pupils in mainstream schools may be removed to these units where, because of high levels of staffing, their *behaviour* may be contained and improved. Some units are housed in separate premises; others may be located in schools. The intention is to provide appropriate conditions for improving behaviour before pupils return to ordinary schools but, in practice, some pupils have to complete compulsory schooling in the units. See *behavioural problems; bullying; discipline; emotional and behavioural difficulties (EBD).*

dissertation   The dissertation is a formal, extended written submission (for a qualification) in which the candidate is expected to treat the subject in a systematic way at a suitable intellectual level. In some institutions, dissertation and *thesis* may not be interchangeable; the thesis, for example, may prove more demanding in depth, range and argument.

distance learning   With the advent of the *Open University* in 1969, distance learning was greatly extended and refined in this country. In essence, it is home study based on the correspondence course, supplemented by audio and video tapes and radio and television programmes. The materials are largely self-instructional and the home institution may also schedule a supporting programme of tutorials. It is anticipated that recent advances in television technology – especially satellite and cable communications – will extend and enhance distance learning in the very near future. See *adult education; continuing education; educational television; National Extension College (NEC); Open College of the Arts*.

Down's syndrome (mongolism)   Langdon Down, a nineteenth-century doctor, gave his name to the syndrome. He described patients who had similar physical characteristics – snub nose, narrow eyes, flattened cheeks, stubby fingers – and who appeared to be mentally retarded. Current thinking suggests that the condition is linked to irregularities in chromosomes. Pupils who have the condition may have to be catered for in *special schools* but many are now educated in mainstream classes. See *learning difficulty; special educational needs (SEN)*.

dual system   The dual system allows for the coexistence of *state* and *church schools* in England and Wales. Duality was established under the 1870 Education Act and in 1902 a further Act allowed rate aid (i.e. funding from local rates) to church schools in return for local authorities' nominees as managers (of schools) and oversight of the curriculum (excluding religious aspects). Arrangements were altered further by the 1944 Act when *voluntary schools* entered into new financial agreements with the authorities and assumed status as either aided or controlled or special; status depended on the nature of the chosen agreement.

Duke of Edinburgh Award   The scheme was founded in 1956 and was intended to afford opportunities for young people to discover their talents, develop character and become socially aware – particularly in the service of others. Awards at three levels – bronze, silver and gold – can be pursued by those between 14 and 25 years of age; each of the three levels is divided into four sections: physical recreation; skills; service to community; expeditions. The scheme operates through associations or groups for young people and information is usually available from local authorities. See *community service*. For further information contact:

Duke of Edinburgh Award Scheme
Gulliver House
Madeira Walk
Windsor
Berks
SL4 1EU

Telephone No: 01753 810753

dyslexia   Dyslexia, sometimes referred to as word-blindness, is often used as a blanket term to cover different, but related, disorders in learning to read and write. There are no consensus views on causes or definition but there is general agreement that the condition can have very serious consequences in schooling generally and in achievement in particular. Dyslexic pupils, it is argued, can sometimes be identified by such things as confused left to right orientation; inability to follow a sequence of instructions; physical clumsiness and poor fluency. See *backwardness; late developers; learning difficulty; special educational needs (SEN)*. For further information contact:

British Dyslexia Association
98 London Road
Reading
Berks
RG1 5AU

Telephone No: 01734 668271

~ E ~

Economic and Industrial Understanding (EIU)   This is one of the cross-curricular themes of the *National Curriculum*. The idea of EIU is that children of all ages will begin to develop an understanding of the way industry works. This might involve *school visits*, games and simulations, job shadowing or forming school companies of various kinds. See *business education*.

Economic and Social Research Council (ESRC)   The Social Science Research Council (SSRC) was superseded by ESRC in 1983, the current responsible body for funding of research in education in universities and institutions of higher education. For further information contact:

> Economic and Social Research Council
> Polaris House
> North Star Avenue
> Swindon
> SN2 1UJ
>
> Telephone No: 01793 413000

Education Association (EA)   A school perceived to be 'at risk' (i.e. not providing an adequate education) following inspection and submission of a governors' action plan, may be taken over and managed by an EA, the members of which are appointed by the *Secretary of State for Education*. The EA will manage the school until the Secretary is satisfied with the school's performance and, in the long term, may consider changing its status to *grant maintained* (GM).

education committee   This is a committee of elected councillors responsible for the council's education service. The committee meets regularly at the town or county hall and consults with, and receives reports from, its *Chief Education Officer* or Director of Education.

Education Reform Act (ERA) 1988   The Act created *open enrolment*, compelled schools to publish information about themselves and introduced *grant maintained schools* (GMS) and the *National Curriculum*. See *Schools Examination and Assessment Authority (SEAC); Standing Advisory Council on Religious Education (SACRE); statutory order.*

Education Secretary   See *Secretary of State.*

Education Support Grant (ESG)   The Grant is controlled and awarded by central government and is specifically intended for improvement in educational provision. Activities or projects which the *Secretary of State* for Education deems important are made known and *local education authorities* are encouraged to make bids. There is then competition between schools for the additional funding and, in the event, there are winners and losers.

Education Welfare Officer (EWO)   EWOs are employed by *local education authorities* through the Education Welfare Service and are usually allocated to a school or schools. They work closely with teachers when dealing with pupils' welfare and brief parents in cases of non-attendance, *exclusion,* suspension or *truancy.* They may be involved, too, in dealing with cases of *child abuse.* Their task, therefore, is to assist both schools and parents to overcome social and educational factors likely to have adverse effects on children's schooling.

Educational Institute of Scotland (EIS)   The EIS is the representative body for most teachers in primary and secondary schools and in further education colleges in Scotland. The Institute, through its committees, negotiates salaries and conditions on behalf of members. For further information contact:

Educational Institute of Scotland
46 Moray Place
Edinburgh
EH3 6BH

Telephone No: 0131 225 6244

educational psychologists   *School psychological services*, normally operating within *local education authorities*, exist to provide specialist information on pupils giving schools cause for concern. Educational psychologists have worked as teachers and then undertaken a postgraduate course of study to enable them to work as psychologists within the education service. They are called upon to provide assessments of individual children. Often, though not exclusively, such assessment will be within *statementing* procedures for children with *learning difficulties*. See *behavioural problems; child guidance; diagnostic assessment; disruptive units; family therapy; special educational needs (SEN).*

Educational Resources Information Centre (ERIC) The Educational Resources Information Centre is an American venture engaged in disseminating information about research through its monthly journal 'Resources in Education' containing abstracts. It is an important source of reference for research students at all levels. For further information contact:

Educational Resources Information Centre
US Department of Education
Office of Educational Research and Improvement
Washington DC 20208
USA

Telephone No: 00 1 202 254 5500

educational television Educational television programmes are made or commissioned by both the BBC and ITV companies to support and extend learning in schools and colleges. In a broader sense, the term can also include programmes intended for adult learners – e.g. *Open University* students – and documentaries. See *adult education; continuing education; distance learning; open learning.*

educationally subnormal (ESN) Some teachers and educationalists dislike the term because, in their view, it is negative and pejorative. Subnormality usually implies intellectual impairment, categorised as either M (moderate) or S (severe), and is often accompanied by physical or emotional handicaps. In cases of severe, multiple handicap, children may need continuous care. See *learning difficulty; screening; statement; special educational needs (SEN).*

efficiency (of school) Efficiency is generally applied to *budget* arrangements. These arrangements may be dependent on local circumstances. With few exceptions, *maintained* primary and secondary *schools* now have *delegated budgets*, funded by *formula* through the *LEAs* since April 1994 (or earlier in some areas). Direct funding of *grant maintained schools* (GMS) is the responsibility of the *Funding*

Agency for Schools (FAS), a *quango* established in April 1994. In all schools, budgets must be accepted, and monitored, by governing bodies and they must ensure that proper accounts are kept. In GM schools, *bursars* or other responsible members of administrative staff work closely with *governors* in monitoring expenditure. If, for any reason, there is no delegated budget, school governors are furnished with accounts by the LEAs. See *accountability*.

elementary school   Before the enactment of the 1944 Education Act, the elementary school catered for pupils in the 5 to 14 age range. The Act ensured a uniform pattern of schooling – *primary* education for all from 5 to 11 years of age (followed by *secondary*). See *three Rs*.

eleven-plus examination   This *examination* was organised by *local education authorities* as a *selection* test for placing 11-year-olds in secondary schools.

emotional and behavioural difficulties (EBD)   EBD is used in connection with the educational provision made for pupils who have severe difficulties or disorders. See *behavioural problems*; *child guidance*; *disruptive units*; *special educational needs (SEN)*; *special schools*.

encyclopaedism   See *essentialism*.

end of key stage statements (EKSS)   These are formal, statutory statements relating to achievement normally expected by the end of *key stages* in the *National Curriculum* (NC). The statements indicate the *knowledge*, *skills* and understanding which pupils, at different stages of maturity and *ability*, should be able to demonstrate.

English as a foreign language (EFL)   EFL is used specifically in the United Kingdom to categorise the teaching of English to foreigners. ESOL (English for speakers of other languages) is a wider term; it includes the teaching of English to foreigners *and* the teaching of English as a second language. See *language schools*.

entrance awards   These awards are made to certain successful candidates in entrance examinations conducted by some universities, colleges, private and public schools. Oxford and Cambridge, for example, offer *scholarships* and exhibitions. Awards can be open or closed; the former is based on a straightforward order of merit and the latter is usually confined to a subject or to candidates from a specified school or college. See *Assisted Places Scheme*.

emeritus   As a title, emeritus is sometimes bestowed on retiring *professors* or readers in recognition of their work or service to their *universities*. See *honorary degree*.

Equal Opportunities Commission (EOC)   Under legislation enacted in 1970 (Equal Pay Act) and 1975 (Sex Discrimination Act plus subsequent amendments in 1986), there should be no discrimination against particular groups in education or employment. Under Sections 53–61 and Schedule 3 of the 1975 Act, the EOC is empowered to foster good practice and monitor the working and effects of legislation.

Many schools, colleges and universities now embrace equal opportunities policies but the existence of policies does not always ensure the elimination of sexual or racial discrimination. See *hidden curriculum; race; sexism*. For further information contact:

> The Equal Opportunities Commission
> Overseas House
> Quay Street
> Manchester
> M3 3HN
>
> Telephone No: 0161 833 9244

essentialism   Philosophers might argue that essentialism is a Platonic theory to justify the meaningful existence of ideal form. In education, the term is used to imply that there is essential *knowledge* that all pupils or students need to master in an encyclopaedic way. Encyclopaedism or essentialism, therefore, may lead to strong centralism in curriculum and control of compulsory schooling.

ethnic minority   These are pupils from particular ethnic heritages, for example those of Asian heritage from Bangladesh, Pakistan, India or East Africa, those of African or Caribbean heritage, or those of Chinese heritage. Many pupils in ethnic minorities have been born in the United Kingdom. Minorities are often associated with countries in the British (New) Commonwealth, although non-Commonwealth refugee pupils may also be found in schools. See *compensatory education; deficit model; language deficit; multicultural education; race; Rampton Report; Section 11 staff*.

evaluation   This is the process through which the worthwhileness and effectiveness of a training or education course is established. A strategy for evaluation may be based on qualitative and/or quantitative approaches. Thus, students or pupils may be asked to rate or comment on the *quality* and relevance of a course. See *developmental testing; feedback; formative; summative assessment*.

evening classes   These classes are usually held in *local education authority* centres, *further education* centres and *community colleges*. The classes cover a wide range of educational and leisure topics and are open to all people (16+ and older) in the community. See *adult education; community education; continuing education; extra-mural studies*.

examining   This is one mode of *assessing* and is normally conducted under controlled conditions. The examination is based on written or oral questions; in its most common form, it consists of a written question paper to which candidates write answers within a given period of time. See *continuous assessment; differentiated examinations; limited grade examination; mock examination; oral; pass mark; pass rate; Schools Examination and Assessment Council (SEAC); testing*.

exchange schemes   Sometimes schools will take the initiative in arranging a scheme whereby a party from one school will visit another country, stay in the homes of pupils of the same age and engage in a variety of educational, cultural, sporting and social activities. The exchange visit will take place, in reverse, later. A different version of an exchange scheme might include a more individual programme designed to assist more directly in learning a foreign language.

exclusion   The *headteacher* may exclude a pupil or pupils who seriously breach the school's disciplinary code. The power to exclude temporarily or permanently is derived from Section 22 of the Education (No. 2) Act 1986; three categories of exclusion, namely fixed term, indefinite or permanent, were clarified. Section 261 of the 1993 Education Act subsequently abolished indefinite exclusion and limited fixed period exclusions to 15 days in any one term. DFE Circular 10/94 draws attention to compliance of both LEA-*maintained schools* and *self-governing (GM)* schools in these matters. In addition, it details the roles of the headteacher, *governing body* and *local education authority*, outlines the procedures to be followed, and affirms that funding should follow the pupil who is permanently excluded into the alternative educational provision. See *behaviour; discipline; Education Welfare Officer (EWO)*.

extended day   The extended day is operated by schools that wish to remain open after normal school hours in order to offer *extra-curricular activities* or facilities for *homework*. See *after-school activities; school day*.

extra-curricular activities   The activities, planned and supervised by teachers or responsible adults, take place outside the normal curricular *timetable*. They may take place before or after school hours, during lunchtimes, at weekends or in holidays. See *after-school activities; exchange scheme; extended day; field study; school day; school visit*.

extra-mural studies   These studies are provided by a university department for the public. They may be offered through *evening classes*, day schools or weekend or summer schools and can lead to sub-degree qualifications. See *adult education; community education; continuing education; further education*.

~ F ~

faculty   A group of *departments* in secondary schools is sometimes formed into a faculty. The Head of Faculty will generally be a senior member of the *school management team*. See *head of department*.

falling rolls   The roll of the school refers to the total number of its pupils. A falling roll indicates a reducing intake of pupils, year by year, leading to a reduced *budget* and, ultimately, fewer teachers and facilities. See *capitation*; *forms of entry*.

family grouping   This is a way of grouping children of several ages in one *class*, rather than having all children of the same age. It is commonly used as a way of grouping in small schools, where single-age classes are impossible to arrange. See *mixed-age class*; *vertical grouping*.

family groups   Family groups of schools are groups in a neighbourhood, generally *primary schools*. They might get together into school clusters to plan a shared programme of *in-service education* or a common approach to *teacher training*, for example.

family therapy   The problems of an individual child may be rooted in the family. It may sometimes be recommended that the family as a whole is given help to acknowledge problems and better understand what is causing them through the process of group *counselling* termed family therapy. The idea is that if therapy helps the family to overcome its difficulties and improve relationships, all the individuals within that family will benefit. See *behavioural problems*; *child guidance*; *educational psychologists*; *emotional and behavioural difficulties (EBD)*.

feedback   This is a term commonly used to indicate the information pupils receive from teachers, verbally or in writing, on some aspects of their performance in school. See *continuous assessment*; *developmental testing*; *evaluation*; *reports*.

feeder school   A feeder school 'feeds' pupils to a school at a subsequent educational stage. A *secondary school*, for example, will have several feeder *primary schools*.

field study   Pupils' work in schools commonly includes work in the local or more distant environment related to their school subjects. A field trip is an expedition to such a locality to undertake field studies. Such studies are regular features of work in history, geography and science. They might include work on a local street, a visit to a castle or to a pond or nature reserve. See *extra-curricular activities; school visit*.

first school   Some *local education authorities* restructured their educational provision into first and *middle schools* following the *Plowden Report* (1967). First schools cater for children aged 5 to 8 whilst middle schools normally take children aged 8 to 12. The rationale for this form of schooling was that it more closely mirrored discrete stages of children's social and intellectual development. Since the 1988 Education Act there has been a move away from first and middle schools and a reinstatement of conventional transfer from the *infant* to a *junior* stage at 7 and to a *secondary* stage at 11. See *age of transfer; primary schools; transition*.

flashcards   These are cards with letters, groups of letters, words or phrases which may be 'flashed' in front of individual children or groups of children as part of the process of teaching them to read. See *reading*.

form   This is a group of children in a school. The term is most often used in a *secondary school*. In *primary schools* children are more commonly said to be grouped in *classes*.

formative   The term formative is used to describe an approach to *assessment* or *evaluation* (formative assessment, formative evaluation) which is ongoing, happens during a course of study and is intended to influence and improve teachers' teaching and pupils' learning. It is generally contrasted with *summative assessment* or summative evaluation which assesses pupil's learning or evaluates a course of study at its conclusion. See *continuous assessment*.

forms of entry   This describes the number of *forms* (of 30 pupils approximately) which a *secondary school* takes into its intake year. From this can be estimated the size of the intake year and the size of the school. See *capitation; falling rolls*.

formula funding   This is the formula, related to the number and age of pupils, which is used to determine the amount of funding a school receives. See *budget*; *capitation*; *standard spending assessment (SSA)*.

foundation course   Some courses of study offer a foundation course, unit or *module* which provides students with a basic introduction to the *concepts*, *skills* and terminology they will need to complete successfully the whole programme. In some foundation courses there is often an emphasis on improving students' *study skills*.

foundation subjects   These are the ten subjects of the *National Curriculum*. Three of these are the *core subjects* – English, mathematics and science. The other seven foundation subjects are history, geography, technology, music, art, physical education and a modern foreign language.

free periods   These are periods of the school day when pupils and teachers are free from a *timetabled* class. Free periods are not available for pupils in primary schools and are extremely rare for teachers. In secondary schools pupils do get some free periods, more frequently in post-16 programmes, when they are normally expected to engage in private study. Teachers' free periods are more common, but by no means generously available, in the secondary school. Most teachers use free periods for administration, preparation or marking. See *contact ratio*; *non-contact time*.

free school   A small number of schools offer free school programmes for parents who want an alternative to mainstream schools. The idea of free schools was influenced by Ivan Illich, especially his 1971 book 'Deschooling Society'. See *de-schooling*.

full course   This is a course derived from the *National Curriculum* and arranged according to a *programme of study* (PoS) and *attainment targets* (ATs) for a particular subject or subjects.

full-time (FT)   Full-time (FT) refers to teachers or other members of staff who are contracted to work for agreed full hourages with related conditions.

full-time equivalent (FTE)   This is a term which can apply to students or teachers. In *further* and *higher education*, where many students study *part-time*, a count of student numbers is often made in full-time equivalence where, for example three students on a part-time course may count as one FTE. In staffing there is a move to appoint staff on part-time or fractional appointments and, comparatively rarely, to share a job. Thus, full-time equivalence is a statistical device used to quantify levels of staffing which include full-time and part-time staff; for example a total of 35 full- and part-time members of staff might have an FT equivalence of 31.4 FTE for *timetabling* or other administrative purposes. See *teacher–class ratio*.

Funding Agency for Schools (FAS)   The agency is a *quango* set up by the *Education Secretary* in April 1994 to oversee matters relating to *grant maintained schools* (GMS) and the provision of school places. The agency, headed by Sir Christopher Benson, is based in York and Darlington, has a board of 12 members, a staff of 190 and is responsible to the Education Secretary and the House of Commons Public Accounts Committee, not directly to parents. It will provide annual reports on its work, the first of which will be published by August 1995.

The agency is empowered to take over control of schooling in *LEAs* in which 75 per cent or more of pupils attend GM schools. In areas in which a minimum 10 per cent of pupils attend GM schools, school planning is shared between the agency and the LEAs.

When it began operating in April 1994, the agency shared responsibility for planning with three authorities for primary places and with 42 authorities for secondary places; in two other authorities, Brent and Hillingdon, it assumed overall responsibility for secondary places. The main duties of the agency are as follows:

- the calculation and transfer of appropriate funding to GM schools (i.e. recurrent and special grants and loans);
- monitoring of GM schools' finances (which will include value for money exercises);
- overseeing the provision of school places.

For further information contact:

Funding Agency for Schools
Albion Wharf
25 Skeldergate
York
YO1 2XL

Telephone No: 01904 661 662

further education (FE)   There are more than four hundred institutions providing post-16 courses for school leavers. Most of these specialise in *vocational education* of various kinds, although the range of study is wide and includes some non-vocational elements. Some FE colleges offer some *higher education* courses too, often in cooperation with *universities* which franchise parts of their *degree* courses. See *Further and Higher Education Act (1992)*; *Further Education Unit (FEU)*; *tertiary college*.

Further Education Funding Council (FEFC)   See *Further and Higher Education Act (1992)*.

Further Education Unit (FEU)   The Unit collects information about, and advises on, the *further education* sector. It is interested in raising *quality* and *standards* through flexibility in learning and conducts research projects. For further information contact:

> Further Education Unit
> Citadel Place
> Tinworth Street
> London
> SE11 5EH
>
> Telephone No: 0171 962 1280

Further and Higher Education Act (1992)   This 1992 Act made *further education* institutions independent corporations, cutting them loose from local authority control. Their funding is derived from the Further Education Funding Council (FEFC), operating in a similar way to bodies such as the University Grants Committee, the National Advisory Board, the Polytechnics and Colleges Funding Committee and the *Higher Education Funding Council* which distributed funds to *higher education*. The other main feature of the Act was the provision for polytechnics to adopt the title of *university*. This ended the so-called *binary* divide in higher education and a more broadly-based university system was established.

~ G ~

General Certificate of Education (GCE)   The Ordinary (*O*) and Advanced *(A) level* examinations of the GCE came into being in 1951 as replacements for the *School Certificate* and Higher School Certificate. See *Advanced Supplementary GCE (AS); S level; university entrance requirements.*

General Certificate of Secondary Education (GCSE)   The GCSE was introduced in 1988 to replace the former *General Certificate in Education* (GCE) and *Certificate in Secondary Education* (CSE). It is the examination taken by the vast majority of the school population at the end of compulsory schooling at 16. It is the chief form of assessment of the *National Curriculum* at the end of *key stage* 4. It is an external examination, set and moderated by independent examination boards.

General National Vocational Qualification (GNVQ)   The GNVQ, introduced in 1992, is a one-year full-time course for post-16 students in school or further education. It is intended as a broadly-based vocational alternative to *A level* and planned as a course which bridges academic and vocational elements. See *Diploma of Vocational Education (DVE); National Vocational Qualifications (NVQ); Royal Society of Arts (RSA).*

General Schools Budget (GSB)   This is the total amount of spending (direct and indirect) on *LEA maintained schools* provided by central government. See *budget.*

General Teaching Council (GTC)   There has been a long campaign to establish a GTC in England and Wales. A GTC was established in Scotland in 1965. The functions are to regulate entry to the profession, advise on training and maintain professional *standards*. See *College of Preceptors.*

gifted children The idea of giftedness refers to children with special *abilities*. Normally this is thought of in terms of unusually high *intelligence* although giftedness might also refer to special talent in the arts, music or sport. An area of debate is the extent to which gifted children are more likely to thrive in the company of other gifted children and therefore how far there should be special, separate provision for them. For further information contact:

National Association for Gifted Children
Park Campus
Boughton Green Road
Northampton
NN2 7AL

Telephone No: 01604 792300

girls' education See *single-sex schools*.

Girls' Public Day School Trust (GPDST) The Trust was established four years after the Taunton Report of 1868 revealed that there were few suitable schools for girls. The Trust continues to promote the interests of girls' public day schools. For further information contact:

GPDST
26 Queen Anne's Gate
London
SW1H 9AN

Telephone No: 0171 222 9595

Girls' Schools Association (GSA) See *Headmaster's Conference* (HMC).

governors The composition and responsibilities of the governing bodies of *maintained schools* are governed by the 1986 Education Act and, in the case of *GM schools*, by the 1988 Act. The duties and powers of governing bodies, and the division of functions between them, *headteachers* and *LEAs*, vary according to whether a school is a county or controlled school, an aided or special agreement school, a maintained *special school*, or a grant maintained school. Guidance for each of these categories is given in the appropriate edition of the *DFE* publication 'School Governors: A Guide to the Law'.

Under the articles of government, the governors of county, voluntary and maintained special schools have a general responsibility for the conduct of the school, acting within the requirements of the legislation. GM schools have a parallel responsibility. The articles of government also list any responsibilities which have been delegated to the governing body by the LEA in the case of county, voluntary and maintained special schools, and the *Secretary of State* in the case of GM schools. The head is responsible for the day-to-day running of the school in accordance with the governors' policies and guidance. Governors are entitled to receive certain categories of information from the head and the LEA and must themselves supply certain information to parents, the head, the DFE and the LEA. They must report annually in writing to parents and must hold an annual meeting to which all parents are invited. They may also have powers concerning the *admission* of pupils or, if not, must be consulted by the LEA about its admission policy.

The governing body has responsibilities in relation to curricular policies including that for *sex education* and for appropriate provision for pupils with *special educational needs*. It plays a major role in pupils' *discipline* and *attendance*, and has responsibilities, which vary depending on the type of school, for school premises. Where the *budget* is delegated from the LEA, the governing body controls its allocation, including the discretionary elements of teachers' pay, and must keep accurate accounts. In those schools with *delegated budgets* the governing body has important powers and duties in the appointment, dismissal and discipline of staff which apply even where, as in the case of county and controlled schools, the teachers are actually employed by the LEA. See *instrument of government*; *lay inspector*; *local management of schools (LMS)*; *National Association for Governors and Managers (NAGM)*; *parent governors*.

grades Terminology surrounding grades as a part of educational *assessment* is sometimes elusive. Put simply, a grade is a numerical or literal mark signifying a level of achievement. In order to arrive at such a judgement, markers commonly refer to grade descriptions (a model of an expected response) or grade criteria (indicators of performance at different levels). Graded *tests* are designed to show the level of student achievement in a subject by a progression of more difficult questions. The wider idea of graded assessment refers to the notion of designing an assessment system flexible enough to meet students' individual learning *objectives*. See *limited grade examination*; *teachers' ratings*.

graduate A person who has successfully completed a course of study at first *degree* level, for example a BA or BSc, is a graduate. Most degree programmes validated by British *universities* take three years of full-time study to complete.

grammar schools   The history of grammar schools stretches back to the middle ages. The grammar school originally taught a classical curriculum and the tradition continued with the nineteenth-century version of a *liberal* education. In the twentieth century the future of grammar schools was strengthened by the 1902 and 1944 Education Acts. By the 1960s the practice of selecting pupils for admission to grammar schools by the competitive *11+ examination* was under attack. In the main, grammar schools have been replaced by *comprehensive schools* which cater for all abilities. However, some former *direct grant* grammar schools became *independent* schools and a small minority of *local education authorities* continued to maintain grammar schools. Some commentators see the creation of *grant maintained status* (GMS) under the 1988 Education Act as a device to facilitate the re-creation of selective grammar schools. See *bilateral school; bipartite system; high school; secondary school; tripartite system.*

grant maintained schools (GMS)   The 1988 *Education Reform Act* introduced the idea of grant maintained status, or *opting out* of local authority control. Grant maintained schools remain within the *state* sector but receive their money direct from the *Department for Education* whose responsibility they became.

   Grant maintained schools determine which children they will accept as pupils and on what basis. They are an essential part of the government's policy of providing a more diverse educational system and one which raises educational standards. The policy is criticised by those who see the GMS sector as irrelevant to the needs of the majority of children and as receiving preferential funding. The *budget* received by GM schools is theirs to spend as they wish, defining a school's priorities locally in line with parental preference and children's needs. See *Annual Maintenance Grant (AMG); Funding Agency for Schools (FAS); local education authority (LEA); local management of schools (LMS); magnet schools; maintained schools; management.* For further information contact:

The Grant Maintained Schools Centre
Wesley Court
4a Priory Road
High Wycombe
Buckinghamshire
HP13 6SE

Telephone No: 01494 474470

The Grant Maintained Schools Foundation
36 Great Smith Street
London
SW1P 3BU

Telephone No: 0171 233 4666

grants   The value of student grants has diminished substantially over recent years. It is still the case that the amount of grant received depends upon parental income. As the number of students going on to *higher education* has increased, so the government has sought to decrease the amount of grant it pays overall. A system of student loans has been developed to help offset the fall in the level of student support through grants. See *bursary*; *designated course*; *discretionary award*; *maintenance grant*; *mandatory award*; *specific grants*.

Grants for Education Support and Training (GEST)   These are provided in block grants by central government to support *in-service education* organised by *LEA*s. There have been a number of similar schemes over the years for government-defined in-service training. The GEST scheme is specifically concerned with priorities for in-service training related to the implementation of the *National Curriculum*. Monies are granted for specific areas, such as assessment, the development of subject knowledge or the development of curriculum coordinators' skills. Grants are also available for expenditure on books, equipment and *ancillary staff* in areas specified for development.

graphicacy   This is an ability to think in a visual way, with good *spatial* awareness. The term is intended to evoke the same kind of meaning for the visual sphere as terms like *literacy* and *numeracy* do in their spheres.

group moderation   This is a *moderation* process, usually undertaken by a number of teachers from neighbouring schools, who meet to standardise each others' ratings so that they conform to national *standards*. See *teachers' ratings*.

group size   Every school is given a group number, from one to six, depending on its size. The salaries of headteachers are related to the group size of the school.

groupwork   This is a way of organising pupils in which the teacher assigns tasks to groups of children. The tasks are undertaken collectively, although the work is often completed on an individual basis. See *collaborative/cooperative groupwork*.

guidance This is a process of support in which pupils are helped by teachers acting in a *pastoral* capacity to deal constructively with the variety of factors which may influence their personal, educational and vocational development. The class teacher in primary schools and form or year tutor in secondary schools are the most common sources of guidance in school settings. See *careers advice and guidance; counselling; health education; moral education; personal and social education (PSE); spiritual, moral, social and cultural development*.

half-term This is a break in teaching, ranging from two or three days to a week, in the middle of each *term*.

halo effect This is a term which explains how a previous judgment about a pupil's *ability* tends to be confirmed in subsequent judgements. There is a tendency to view the halo effect as mainly operating when pupils are performing well but it can also operate by confirming low levels of *attainment*. See *labelling; self-fulfilling prophecy*.

Hawthorne effect This refers to the effect of observers on the performance of those who are observed. The origin of the term is an experiment about industrial efficiency in the Hawthorne works near Chicago. Operatives who were observed increased their output. The implication for education is that introducing new systems or curricula, or engaging in evaluation studies or research, can lead to change or improvement which may be temporary.

head of department This is a term which usually applies to senior teachers in *secondary schools*. A head of *department* is responsible for the organisation and leadership of a subject area in a school, leading the staff who teach that subject. There will be meetings to call, policies to agree and systems to put in place to deal with all facets of the teaching of that subject within the school. In some larger schools there may be heads of *faculty*, responsible for a group of subjects, such as history, English and religious studies within a faculty of humanities. Faculty heads are likely to be members of the senior *management* team of the school. See *dean; school management team*.

Head Start This is a United States' nursery programme intended to develop the learning potential of *disadvantaged* children. It entailed the transfer of resources to areas of social disadvantage in a programme of *compensatory education*. Head Start rests on the belief that early learning experiences have great power for the individual's future development and life opportunities. See *positive discrimination; pre-school education*.

Headmasters' Conference (HMC) The Conference dates from 1869 when Edward Thring of Uppingham and others sought to voice limited opposition to the Endowed Schools Commission's enquiries. The Conference still exists as an influential forum for discussion and action in promoting common interests. Membership bestows status on *headteachers* and prestige on their schools. See *public schools*.

headteacher The headteacher has overall responsibility for the work of the school. The extent of the responsibility is the same whether the head is working in a small primary school or a large secondary school. In other words the head's responsibility includes staff deployment and development, school organisation, financial *management* and implementation of the *National Curriculum*. However, the complexity of the role is clearly related to organisational size and management structures will reflect this. Headteachers increasingly voice the need for more training in management skills and there have been limited moves to meet training needs since the 1988 *Education Reform Act*. It is important for the headteacher to establish effective working relations with the school's governing body. See *deputy head; discipline; governors; Headmasters' Conference (HMC); local management of schools (LMS); National Association of Headteachers (NAHT); principal; public schools; school management team; Secondary Heads Association (SHA)*.

health education A school's concern for the health of its children will be evident in various ways and a school policy may well spell these out. It might include consideration of the role models children observe, including teachers. It may involve the kind of food available in school, curriculum projects which emphasise healthy living, including aspects of diet and exercise. A well-rounded PE programme will include a concern for children's health. Within science, increasingly, more specialised inputs will apply, including aspects of personal hygiene and behaviour. The school governing body is responsible for identifying the school's stance on *sex education*. See *counselling; guidance; pastoral care; personal and social education (PSE); school health service*.

Her Majesty's Inspectorate (HMI) The initial function of HMI in the nineteenth century was to report on educational provision, particularly in respect of its cost-effectiveness. HMI are appointed by

Order in Council and so the service is independent of government. Their role, increasingly, developed into the collecting and synthesising of information about aspects of the national education service as well as the undertaking of individual school inspections. Under the terms of the 1992 Education (Schools) Act the focus shifted to more regular school inspections undertaken by largely privatised *inspection teams*. HMI's role now includes training new *inspectors* and *monitoring* the quality of work undertaken by the privatised teams. See *Office for Standards in Education; Office of Her Majesty's Chief Inspector of Schools (OHMCI); registered inspector*.

hidden curriculum   The term was coined to identify all those school experiences which influence children beyond the formal structure of the taught *curriculum*. It may be argued that the total experience of schooling – encompassing, for example, decisions about pupil groupings, attitudes to *equal opportunities* and patterns of social relationships among pupils – has a profound effect on pupil learning. Clearly these hidden, or implicit, features of school life figure prominently in a child's view of his or her place in school. See *race; sexism*.

high school   A term which is in little use today. It has been used by *grammar schools* and some *independent* 11–18 all-through schools. Where it is still in use, it most commonly denotes the lower years of a *secondary school*, especially where the *lower school* occupies a separate site.

higher degree   Most teachers now have a first *degree*, that is a degree at Bachelor level, for example BA, BSc or BEd. Formerly teachers routinely qualified with a Certificate in Education (Cert Ed), from a two- and later three-year training programme. An increasing number of teachers now study for an additional, higher degree, usually through part-time study. The most common of these higher degrees is the Master of Arts (MA) or Master of Education (MEd) award. A much smaller number will go on to undertake further, more specialised *postgraduate study* at doctoral level, leading to the award of the DPhil or PhD. Such a research programme normally takes three years' full time and five to seven years of part-time study. See *Postgraduate Certificate of Education (PGCE); teacher training*.

higher education (HE)   Courses in higher education lead to awards of *degrees* or higher qualifications. The courses are usually taught in *universities*, which have powers to award their own degrees, or in affiliated institutions. Under the *Further and Higher Education Act*

(1992), HE and FE were amalgamated to form one sector. See *Association for Colleges (AFC)*; *binary system*; *Council for National Academic Awards (CNAA)*; *Robbins Report*; *UCAS*.

Higher Education Funding Council England (HEFCE)   This is the body which distributes state money to the institutions of *higher education* in England. It succeeded the University Grants Committee (UGC) and the Polytechnic and Colleges Funding Committee (PCFC) when the *Further and Higher Education Act (1992)* established a new, more integrated higher education system. The process of awarding funds is a complicated one, employing formulae related to the subject being followed and institutions' skill in recruiting students to declared intake targets. There is a similar funding council for Wales. For further information contact:

HEFCE
Northavon House
Coldharbour Lane
Bristol
BS16 1QD

Telephone No: 01272 317317

Higher Education Quality Council (HEQC)   HEQC was formed in 1992 as the *quality* unit of the *university* sector. It organised itself into three divisions: credit and access; quality enhancement and quality audit. The audit division introduced a programme of testing institutions' mechanisms and procedures for ensuring quality of teaching and learning. A small permanent directorate is supported in its work by part-time auditors recruited from the institutions themselves. See *Academic Audit Unit*. For further information contact:

Higher Education Quality Council
344–354 Gray's Inn Road
London
WC1X 8BP

Telephone No: 0171 278 4411

Hillgate Group   This was one of the influential new right *pressure groups* which came to prominence in the 1980s. Its work was influenced by the publication of a series of education *Black Papers* in the 1970s which criticised what was seen as a harmful cult of *progressivism* and informality in British education. Prominent Black Paper contributors like Caroline Cox and Rhodes Boyson were also associated with the publications of the Hillgate Group. The Group pressed for a reassertion of traditional values in education, for example the primacy of subject matter and the need for more didactic teaching.

home education   A small minority of parents choose to educate their children at home, a right established under the provisions of the 1944 Education Act. There may be special reasons for parents to exercise this right, although *local education authorities* have not generally been anxious to promote it.

Home and School Council   This is a grouping of organisations with an interest in relationships between home and school. These are the *Campaign for the Advancement of State Education* (CASE), the *National Association for Primary Education* (NAPE), the *National Confederation of Parent–Teacher Associations* (NCPTA) and the *Advisory Centre for Education* (ACE). For further information contact:

Home and School Council
40 Sunningdale Mount
Ecclesall
Sheffield
S11 9HA

Telephone No: 01742 364181

home–school relations   The relationship between home and school was given prominence in the *Plowden Report* (1967) and the value of a close relationship has been widely recognised. The ideal is taken to be a kind of partnership in which both home and school make strong complementary contributions to the child's learning. In many schools there is considerable emphasis now on the positive part played by *parents*, for example in helping children to read. Home– school relations are sometimes the special responsibility of a senior teacher. It is sometimes appropriate for the school to arrange a home visit to discuss a child's progress with parents. In general the 1988 Education Act has placed emphasis on the provision of certain kinds of *information* for parents by the school. See *National Confederation of Parent–Teacher Associations; open evening; Parent–Teacher Association; parents' evening.*

homework   The regular setting and marking of homework is a normal feature of school life in the *secondary* phase, and increasingly at the top end of the *primary school* too. There is evidence to suggest that a systematic policy for the setting of homework is a significant factor in determining pupil performance in public *examinations*. It is also one of those elements which contributes to a school ethos, reinforcing the idea that schools require pupils to apply themselves consistently to their school work. There are, of course, dangers that pupils will be asked to do too much, distorting family and social life. Many schools now monitor the pattern of homework set more closely than hitherto. There are some indications, however, that schools' ambitions to perform well in examination *league tables* may lead some to expect pupils to do too much work at home. See *continuous assessment; coursework*.

homosexuality   See *Clause 28; sex education*.

honorary degree   An honorary degree is awarded to mark the respect with which an individual is regarded by a *university*. It may be for academic reputation or an outstanding contribution in his/her sphere of life. It does not entail attending a course of study or passing *examinations*. Honorary degrees are awarded at both *graduate* and *postgraduate* levels. See also *emeritus*.

honours degree   Most students at *university* follow a three-year Bachelor's *degree* with honours. A Pass degree is awarded for those who reach a slightly lower standard than honours. The honours degree is normally classified into categories: first class (1); upper second class (2i); lower second class (2ii); third class (3). There is a view that these distinctions at *undergraduate* level are impossible to sustain and justify. It is difficult to argue that an upper second degree has equivalence across a range of subject areas, or within the same subject areas, in all university-level institutions in the United Kingdom. A move has begun to dismantle the honours classification system and instead simply to award unclassified degrees. See *tripos*.

hospital education   When a child is in hospital, arrangements are normally made for education to continue through teachers employed by *local education authorities* to work exclusively in hospitals.

house system   The system originated in *public schools* in which pupils were (and still are) accommodated in boarding houses under housemasters or housemistresses. Today, the system has been widely adopted in *state secondary schools* for *pastoral care* and, in some instances, for academic work. Teachers and *tutor groups*, drawn from the same *year* group or from different year groups, are attached to houses.

humanities   The study of human issues is sometimes referred to as the humane arts. A group of subjects normally regarded as contributing to the study of man in society includes literature, history, religious study and philosophy. In schools and some universities there may be a humanities faculty within which individual subject departments are grouped.

hyperactivity   This is a term used to denote children who show signs of excessive physical movement. These children find it hard to settle and are always active. They show unusual energy and are extremely hard work for parents and teachers. There have been suggestions that some children's hyperactivity may be explained by certain dietary effects. See *behavioural problems; health education*.

~ I ~

impression marking   This refers to an approach to marking which derives from a subjective or impressionistic judgement about the overall quality of the whole piece of work. It relies on an examiner's experience and implicit feel for the quality required of students at certain stages of their development. It is contrasted with attempts at more precision by an analytic approach. An analytic approach normally relies on criteria setting out exactly what is required in a piece of work and a marking scheme in which specified numbers of marks are awarded for certain parts of a response. See *criterion-referenced test*.

in-class support   Pupils who have *special educational needs* may be given in-class support. During particular lessons, a second teacher may give help to such pupils in mainstream classes thus avoiding the need to withdraw them. Withdrawal, it is claimed, can reduce pupils' self-esteem; in-class support allows the pupils to remain with peers for mainstream learning activities. See *learning support*; *Learning Support Service (SLS)*; *partnership teaching*; *peripatetic teacher*; *special support assistant*; *support teachers*.

Incorporated Association of Preparatory Schools (IAPS)   This is an association of *headteachers* of girls' and boys' *preparatory schools* and has more than 500 members. For further information contact:

Incorporated Association of Preparatory Schools (IAPS)
11 Waterloo Place
Leamington Spa
Warwickshire
CV32 5LA

Telephone No: 01926 887833

independent learning   This is an approach to *learning* in which an individual proceeds with a piece of work with minimum support from a teacher. It is becoming common within modular degree programmes in higher education, for example, to include independent learning modules. These are intended to facilitate student-centred inquiry within a defined assessment framework and with some *tutorial* support. See *individual learning*.

independent schools   See *public schools*.

Independent Schools Information Service (ISIS)   This is an information service for parents requiring *information* about the independent education sector. It has a number of regional offices and also conducts research on aspects of independent education. For further information contact:

> Independent Schools Information Service (ISIS)
> 56 Buckingham Gate
> London
> SW1E 6AG
>
> Telephone No: 0171 630 8793/14

individual learning   The term has a range of possible meanings. It can refer to time in class when an individual child is working alone, rather than in groups or as a part of the whole class. It can refer to the teacher's aim of responding to children's learning needs by providing some element of individualisation in the planned *programmes of study*. This may be through the selection of particular learning activities for children, based on an *assessment* of their individual requirements. See *independent learning*.

induction   The term induction refers to the process whereby someone new to a job is helped to become familiar with it. In education the term usually refers to arrangements to support *newly qualified teachers (NQTs)* in their first year in post. A formal *probationary* system, in which *local education authorities* reported to the *Secretary of State* on the performance of beginning teachers in their first year in post, was abandoned in 1992. The replacement is induction, delivered by LEAs and individual schools.

industry   Much attention has been paid to the way in which schools can make a stronger contribution to Britain's economic performance. Over the years a number of attempts have been made to develop closer links between schools and industry. The Schools Council, for example, developed the Schools Council Industry Project (SCIP). The *Technical and Vocational Education Initiative* (TVEI) was introduced in 1982 by the *Manpower Services Commission* (MSC). Its aim was to promote a closer understanding in schools of the skills that industry might require of its future workforce. The *National Curriculum Council* (NCC) promoted *Economic and Industrial Understanding* (EIU) as one of the cross-curricular themes developed within the *National Curriculum* after the 1988 *Education Reform Act*. See *business education; Compact; correspondence theory; Department of Trade and Industry (DTI); work experience*.

infant school   This is a school catering for children between the ages of five and seven, or at *Key Stage* 1 in *National Curriculum* terminology. There may be a separate infant school, or an infant department may be part of a *primary school* catering for children aged five to eleven or the infant stage may be incorporated within a *first school* for children aged from five to eight or nine. Some infant and primary schools may have *nursery classes* or units attached to them. See *reception class; rising fives; transition*.

information   The various educational reforms set in train by the Conservative government in 1988 with the *Education Reform Act* placed great emphasis on the provision of information for *parents* and others. Schools are required to supply the *LEA*, if applicable, and the *Secretary of State* with any information requested. The school *prospectus* has to contain a specified range of information so that parents gain a full picture of the school. Schools are required to make available a range of LEA, government and school documents for public access. The school *governors* must write an annual report which is distributed to parents and must call a meeting at which the report is discussed. The report will explain how the governing body has put its plans into operation in the preceding year. See *accountability; league tables; mission statement; Parents' Charter; performance indicators; records; reports; school policy*.

information technology (IT)   Schools are making increased use of computers as an aid to learning. Information technology is seen as an essential part of children's learning, of relevance to their future lives in a modern society. Within the *National Curriculum* there has been uncertainty about the best way of locating IT, whether it should be seen as a separate subject or something that permeates all subjects or both. It is closely associated with the foundation subject, *design and technology*, although in the *Dearing* consultation in 1994 the proposals for IT were presented separately. Since very slow beginnings in the 1980s, more and better IT equipment has been appearing in schools and more sophisticated software is available.

Inner London Education Authority (ILEA)   As the controlling *LEA* for London, and the largest in the country, ILEA was criticised by the Conservative government for its progressive education policies especially in respect of equal opportunities. It was abolished in 1988 and the 13 London boroughs were established as new LEAs. The argument advanced in favour of the reorganisation was that the smaller LEAs would be more democratically accountable.

in-service education and training (INSET)   In-service education and training is concerned with the development of teachers' professional and academic skills. It can involve relatively short-term activities drawing together the whole staff of a school, for example activities organised as part of school *closure days* (Baker days) and it can involve individual attendance at various kinds of externally arranged courses and conferences. These may be short, one-day events or longer courses such as those organised by and usually held in institutions of higher education. Longer in-service courses normally require part-time evening attendance, usually for one evening a week, over a term, a year, or longer depending on the award associated with a course of study. Teachers commonly enrol on courses at certificate, *diploma* and master's level. Frequently in-service award schemes offered by higher education institutions are part of an integrated modular programme, with a range of flexible pathways through the scheme open to teachers. Since the introduction of the *National Curriculum* the government has sought to support in-service activities in designated areas through a programme of grants to LEAs, the *GEST* programme. See *advisory teacher; block release; day release; higher degree; James Report; postgraduate studies; secondment; staff development; teachers' centres; teacher training; university department of education (UDE)*.

inspection team member   A member is a person who assists a *registered inspector* to conduct the inspection of a school under Section 9 of the Education (Schools) Act 1992. He/she must have completed satisfactorily a course of training provided or approved by Her Majesty's Chief Inspector of Schools (HMCI), unless HMCI waives the requirement. See *Her Majesty's Inspectorate (HMI); lay inspector; Office for Standards in Education (OFSTED); Office of Her Majesty's Chief Inspector of Schools (OHMCI)*.

inspectors   There are three kinds of inspectors who may visit schools from time to time.

Before the 1992 Education Act, only *Her Majesty's Inspectors of Schools* (HMI) made formal inspections of schools. This was work they had undertaken on behalf of the government of the day for more than a hundred years. They may still visit schools as part of particular surveys, or to moderate the work of the new *inspection teams*.

Members of inspection teams may be *registered inspectors* who lead a team; members of inspection teams who have undergone a course of training in inspection methodology; or *lay inspectors* who are not educational professionals and represent the interests of the general public.

Local authority inspectors are personnel employed by *LEAs* as part of their own quality assurance systems. Formerly some LEAs preferred the term adviser, implying a more symbiotic relationship between LEA and school. Since 1988, most LEAs have adopted the title inspector. See *local education authority inspectors*; *Office for Standards in Education (OFSTED)*; *Office of Her Majesty's Chief Inspector of Schools (OHMCI)*.

instruction   Instruction occurs when a learner follows, and is able to do, something he or she has been shown or told by an instructor. Instruction is usually thought of as being less complex than teaching, often involving the learner in imitating a set of *skills* demonstrated by the instructor. Instruction is controlled by the instructor. Training manuals used by instructors sometimes set out the precise stages, timing and terminology involved in the exercise. The processes involved in learning to drive embody the principles of instruction. See *objectives*.

instructor   This is a person who does not have a recognised teaching qualification but who takes some part in instructing pupils or students in *skill*-based areas of learning. Instructors, for example, may take certain *evening classes* in *further education* or make a contribution to the programme open to inmates in *prison*. There has been some discussion of the merits of introducing instructors to schools, under the supervision of fully trained teachers, as a way of generating a more flexible approach to staffing.

instrument of government   All schools have instruments and articles of government which set out the way in which they are managed and what their status is. In effect the instrument is a school constitution, setting out the powers and responsibilities of *governors* and staff. See *law*.

integrated course   This is a course, usually in a secondary school, to which several subjects contribute without retaining their distinct identity (for example integrated humanities, which explores themes which include aspects of geography, history and RE). See *breadth*.

integrated day   This is a form of organisation in which the school day is used to work with primary pupils on a variety of tasks simultaneously rather than all following the same subject at the same time.

integrated work   This is an approach to planning, most frequently in the primary school, based on the idea of an integrated *curriculum*. The idea is that integration of subjects is more useful than treating them separately in *timetabled* subject slots. The form of integration can be through topics, usually in a form of *interdisciplinary* work. In practice most integrated work relates aspects of work from specific subject disciplines rather than fully integrating them. The curriculum of the primary school is also regularly defined as thematic, in other words following a theme in an integrated way. The requirements of the *National Curriculum* have led school planning teams to define more closely the place of subject study in thematic or *topic* work, possibly leading to less integration and more relatedness of subject matter. See *breadth; cross-curricular*.

intelligence   This is a description of mental *ability* or intellectual capacity. The term is riddled with difficulties, not least in resolving the extent to which intelligence is inherited or learned. Intelligence tests have been constructed for many years. The first attempts were made by Alfred Binet (1857–1911) in France and there have been many versions since. An intelligence test attempts to provide a reliable, standardised score of a child's intelligence. The result is known as IQ or *intelligence quotient*, where a score of 100 represents average intelligence. Tests for intelligence were widely used as part of the process of selecting children at 11 for grammar schools. In most cases verbal and non-verbal reasoning tests were given. The tests were sometimes criticised on account of their bias towards particular cultural norms and expectations. See *backwardness; deficit model; eleven-plus examination; gifted children; late developers; meritocracy*.

intelligence quotient (IQ)   IQ is derived from standardised intelligence tests which seek to measure *intelligence* and arrive at a numerical expression of it. In IQ orthodoxy the score 100 is taken as average intelligence. IQ is computed by the formula:

$$\frac{\text{mental age (score in the test)} \times 100}{\text{chronological age} \qquad 1}$$

The idea is that children with high intelligence will have an IQ above 100, those of lower intelligence a score of less than 100. The notion of standardisation is based on the assumption that 66 per cent of the population will fall within the range 85–115.

interdisciplinary   This refers to curriculum planning and provision which cover a range of subject disciplines. Interdisciplinary work is a common approach to planning in the primary school. See *breadth*; *cross-curricular*; *integrated work*; *topic*.

international baccalauréat   See *baccalauréat*.

International Institute for Educational Planning (IIEP)   This is an international centre for the field of educational planning. It was established in 1963 by the *United Nations Educational, Scientific and Cultural Organisation* (UNESCO). For further information contact:

IIEP
UNESCO
7 place de Fontenoy
75352 Paris 07 SP
France

Telephone No: 00 33 1 45 68 10 00

invigilator   This is someone, usually a teacher, who supervises pupils and students when they are sitting *examinations*. The job of the invigilator is to make sure that the examination takes place according to the rules and regulations.

ipsative assessment   A form of *assessment* is termed ipsative when it is determined by the individual learner. The idea is that individuals can set assessment tasks which test learning against individual goals and previous experiences. The term derives from the Latin 'ipse', meaning him or herself.

item   In the terminology surrounding *tests* and *assessment*, an item is a question in an item bank which may be selected by a test conductor when tests are devised.

~ J K ~

James Report Headed by Lord James of Rusholme, the James Report was the result of an inquiry into teacher education and training. It reported in 1972 and proposed a system based on three cycles. First there would be a general education at degree or diploma level, second a full-time course of professional training and third a planned entitlement to regular *in-service education* and training throughout a teacher's career. See *teacher training*.

junior school This is a school for children aged 7 to 11, sometimes standing alone as a separate entity, sometimes incorporated as the junior department of a *primary school*. See *age of transfer*; *first school*; *transition*.

key stage (KS) These are periods in each pupil's education to which the elements of the *National Curriculum* apply. There are four key stages, normally related to the age of the majority of the pupils in a teaching group. They are:

- Key Stage 1, beginning of compulsory education to age 7;
- Key Stage 2, 7 to 11;
- Key Stage 3, 11 to 14;
- Key Stage 4, 14 to end of compulsory education.

The equivalent year groups are:

- Years R (Reception), 1 and 2;
- Years 3 to 6;
- Years 7 to 9;
- Years 10 and 11.

See *coordinator*; *end of key stage statements*; *programme of study*; *short course*; *standard assessment tasks* (SATs); *statement of attainment* (SOA).

kindergarten Literally, this means the 'child's garden' and, applied to education, it means an approach to early years education. It is derived from the ideas of the nineteenth-century teacher, Froebel, and places much emphasis on *play* as a natural way of promoting learning. See *nursery school*; *pre-school education*.

knowledge The philosophical problems of defining knowledge are protracted and well-known but, for students, the general definition is usually characterised by reference to theoretical or practical understanding of a subject. There is, of course, much academic interest in how knowledge is generated and acquired; *Piaget* and Bruner, eminent psychologists, were interested in the stages at which – and processes through which – knowledge can be understood; philosophers such as Hirst, Peters and Phoenix offered explanations for the structure of curricula and educational sociologists drew attention to possible cultural biases of curricula as mediated knowledge of dominant groups in society. See *essentialism*; *learning*.

labelling This is the idea that teachers tend to label pupils according to imprecise and sometimes stereotypical categories (bright, naughty, one-parent family, slow learners). The danger is that the label sticks, becoming a categorisation which the child is unable to shake off or overcome. See *halo effect*; *self-fulfilling prophecy*.

language across the curriculum The *Bullock Report* (1975) recommended that all teachers should regard themselves as teachers of English and that schools should develop policies to ensure systematic approaches when implementing them. Language across the curriculum policies were formulated as responses for all stages of schooling; there was no uniform policy for age phases or schools. Instead, the Committee of Inquiry's recommendations were offered as guidelines for local initiatives. See *deficit model*.

language deficit The belief that pupils may not achieve their potential because of poor command of language is not new. Some educationalists believe that children from working-class and *ethnic minorities* are disadvantaged in learning by their lack of language skills. See *compensatory education*; *deficit model*; *English as a foreign language (EFL)*; *partnership teaching*; *underachievement*.

language laboratory This is an electronically-equipped room designed to help pupils and students to learn languages. The principle of such a laboratory is that students proceed individually and at their own pace using pre-prepared recorded materials.

language schools These are establishments which have been set up to teach pupils and students a second language. There is a large number of independent English language schools, many in London and along the south coast, which attract students from overseas during their own school or college vacation. See *English as a foreign language*.

language support teacher   This is a teacher provided by the LEA or school to enhance language work with a particular group of pupils. See *assistant; bilingual assistants; English as a foreign language (EFL); ethnic minority; language deficit; learning support; partnership teaching; Section 11 staff*.

late developers   Late developers are learners who have lagged behind their peers in learning and have only attained their full potential at a later stage. See *backwardness; dyslexia; intelligence; underachievement*.

law   The law governing the English education system is chiefly statutory and only a few matters remain within the ambit of the common law. The principles on which the school system is founded and the framework within which it functions are mainly to be found in the Education Acts of 1944, 1980, 1981, 1986, the *Education Reform Act 1988* and the Education (Schools) Act 1992. These Acts give the *Secretary of State* for Education the power to make statutory *instruments* (regulations and orders) embodying more detailed legal requirements. The *Department for Education* (DFE) also offers guidance both on the law and on general policy by means of *circular* letters and administrative memoranda. Central government provides the bulk of the finance for the education system but it is largely administered by *local education authorities* (LEAs) and the governing bodies of individual institutions. See *Butler Act (1944 Education Act); statutory order*.

lay inspector   A lay inspector is a member of an *inspection team*, established under the 1992 Education Act, who is without personal experience of educational management in a school or of educational provision. Lay inspectors, however, may be school *governors* or work in schools on a voluntary basis. The purpose of the lay inspector is not to bring specialist expertise to the team, but the perspective of the ordinary member of society. Every inspection team must include a lay inspector. See *inspectors*.

league tables   These lists of school performance in various categories are published as part of *DFE* policy to make schools more accountable and to facilitate parental choice. The league tables simply list raw scores in *rank* order, although there has been belated recognition that some means should be found to take into account particular environmental circumstances relevant to a school's performance. The league tables can measure *attendance*, examination *pass rates*, access to higher education, resource base and staff–student ratios. In practice, the government has shown greatest interest in rates of *truancy* and *examination* performance. See *accountability; information; Parents' Charter.*

learning   A vast literature surrounds the idea of learning and the field of psychology is helpful in exploring it. If the purpose of education is seen as the promotion of learning, then the job of teachers, simplistically, is to ensure that it takes place. There are numerous debates about the conditions in which learning is most likely to occur and the conditions most likely to inhibit it. Different schools of psychologists hold different assumptions and different starting points about learning, leading them to give more or less emphasis to developmental, cognitive, behavioural or social aspects. See *active learning; concept; essentialism; independent learning; instructor; knowledge; mastery learning; memory; motivation; passive learning; problem-solving; programmed learning; rote learning; study skills.*

learning difficulty   A child with a learning difficulty is said to have *special educational needs* (SEN). The imprecise nature of 'learning difficulties' means that there is a huge range of them and many explanations of why they occur. Learning difficulties exist when a child has considerably more difficulty in learning part or parts of the *curriculum* than the majority of pupils of the same age. See *autism; backwardness; diagnostic assessment; disadvantaged; Down's syndrome; dyslexia; educationally subnormal (ESN); educational psychologists; Learning Support Service; Portage scheme; remedial teaching; screening; statement; Warnock Report.*

learning support   This is a means of providing extra help for pupils. The form of support can vary, but commonly includes help through a specialist *support teacher* or the provision of specially designed learning materials. See *in-class support; language support teacher; remedial teaching; Section 11 staff; special support assistants.*

Learning Support Service   This is a team organised by *LEAs* to provide classroom-based support by specialist teachers for pupils experiencing *learning difficulties.* Such a service will also provide advice for schools on the development of their policies for pupils with *special educational needs.* See *in-class support.*

left-handedness   The active discouragement of left-handedness by teachers is now a thing of the past but, in a right-handed world, pupils may need practical advice and guidance when learning to master certain skills such as handwriting.

levels of attainment   The *assessment* of the *National Curriculum* as developed by the *National Curriculum Council* and *SEAC* specified ten different levels of achievement (levels of *attainment*) in relation to every *attainment target* in every subject area. The levels reflected different *standards* as children worked their way through the compulsory curriculum from five to 16. The exceptions were art, music and physical education which did not have attainment levels or *statements of attainment*. The ten-level scale was felt to be difficult to implement and became a part of the focus of the *Dearing* review of the National Curriculum undertaken by the *School Curriculum and Assessment Authority* in 1994.

liberal studies   The idea of liberal education is drawn from the broad curriculum of *trivium* (grammar, logic, rhetoric) and *quadrivium* (astronomy, arithmetic, geometry, music) of mediaeval times. Today, the notion of broadness is retained in contrast with vocationalism and specialisation. In some sixth forms, general studies may be followed to redress a perceived narrowness of *A levels*. See *breadth*; *grammar schools*.

Library Association   The Association was established in 1876 and 22 years later was awarded a Royal Charter. The Association promotes professional development, fosters high standards of public service and provides information and advice for school librarians. See *School Library Association*. For further information contact:

The Library Association
7 Ridgmount Street
London
WC1E 7AE

Telephone No: 0171 636 7543

licensed teacher   The licensed teacher scheme began in 1989. It was one of the ways in which the government sought to open up a diversity of routes in teacher education, giving a greater range of course and training opportunities to candidates interested in training to teach. Its announcement was not universally welcomed on the grounds that it opened up a route whereby non-graduates could become teachers and because it was felt that it would not guarantee the same quality of education and training as received by student teachers following other routes. Licensed teachers are teachers over 24 years of age with academic qualifications beyond A level and generally with experience outside teaching. They are licensed to teach for a period of up to two years. Subject to satisfactory completion of a training programme and successful practice in the classroom the *Secretary of State* can grant *qualified teacher status* (QTS). See *teachers; teacher training*.

limited grade examination This type of *examination* is limited in the sense that marks or *grades* awarded are deliberately confined to part(s) of the whole scale. For example, a particular examination paper tailored to suit pupils of low *ability* might be limited to an upper mark of 50 per cent; on the other hand, a paper intended for those of high ability may take 50 per cent as its lowest acceptable mark. Some papers set for examinations in some *GCSE* subjects are based on this principle.

link course This is usually a *vocational* course, run by two or more educational institutions in a collaborative way.

literacy The attribute of literacy is generally recognised as one of the key educational objectives of compulsory schooling. It refers to the ability to *read* and write at an appropriate level of fluency. See *adult literacy; basic skills; numeracy; oracy; prison education*.

loans See *grants*.

Local Education Authority (LEA) Established under the 1902 Education Act, the LEA was a powerful body in each major area charged with responsibility for education in the compulsory and, in some respects, the post-compulsory years. Education accounts for a large proportion of local expenditure and so the administration of education was a key aspect of local authority services. The LEA's influence was diminished by the 1988 Education Act when schools were given the opportunity to seek independence through *grant maintained* status (GMS). In addition, LEAs lost control of the polytechnics and further education colleges as they achieved independent, corporate status under the *Further and Higher Education Act 1992*. See *appropriate authority; Chief Education Officer (CEO); Council of Local Education Authorities (CLEA); formula funding; Funding Agency for Schools (FAS); General Schools Budget (GSB); Inner London Education Authority (ILEA); maintained schools; opting out; Parents' Charter; Section 12 Notice*.

Local Education Authority (LEA) inspectors These inspectors were formerly advisers who provided advice and planned in-service programmes in their areas. However, since in-service funding was channelled to schools and a pattern of school inspections was established (Education (Schools) Act, 1992), advisers in many authorities have assumed monitoring roles and, like all other inspectors, must tender for contracts to inspect schools. See *inspectors*.

local management of schools (LMS)   Local management of schools (LMS) describes the arrangements whereby *LEAs* delegate to individual schools responsibility for financial and other aspects of *management*.

Each LEA is required to prepare a financial scheme for local management of schools (LMS), with provision for yearly updating (under the 1988 Education Act). Almost all schools received delegated budgetary control by 1994. Schools with a *delegated budget* are funded according to a formula devised by the LEA under the government's guidelines and subject to the *Secretary of State*'s approval. The allocations under the formula vary from LEA to LEA. The formula comprises two main elements:

- the number and ages of the pupils at the school (which determines a minimum of 80 per cent of the aggregated school *budget*);
- other characteristics of the school, for example, the number of pupils with *special educational needs*, disproportionate costs in small schools, school premises factors.

The school's budget includes a minimum cash guarantee for salary costs of staff, day-to-day premises costs, equipment, *resources* and other services used by the school.

So, LMS is the delegation of the management of a school to its local managers, normally the *headteacher* and the *governing* body. It was recognised that the management tasks to be delegated, whilst including financial aspects, were more wide-ranging than budgetary management. See *capitation*; *Education Reform Act 1988*; *grant maintained schools*; *opting out*.

London allowance   Teachers employed in schools within the designated London area are entitled to the allowance to offset the higher costs of working in the capital.

look and say   This approach to the teaching of reading, based upon the recognition of words and phrases, is usually contrasted with an approach through phonics. See *phonics*; *reading*; *reading schemes*.

lower school   This term generally applies to the lower *forms* of a *comprehensive school*, especially when the school operates on *split sites*. It may refer to the lower two or three forms, in other words Years 7 to 9. See *high school*.

~ M ~

magnet school   A magnet school is an inner city school with a high reputation which succeeds in attracting students and parents. Magnet schools tend to specialise in certain vocations or academic specialisms. The term is an American one, specifically used in relation to US attempts to counter inner city deprivation and juvenile crime by high quality educational programmes. Controversy surrounds the idea that the success of magnet schools is achieved only at the cost of other non-magnet schools. The nearest equivalent British experiment is that of the *City Technology College*, which was to some extent based on American experience. The City Technology College is also conceived as a beacon of excellence in inner city communities. The whole movement towards *grant maintained* status could be seen as an attempt to emulate the effect of magnet schools.

maintained schools   These are schools which are funded by the state. Maintained schools therefore include *local education authority* (LEA) schools, *grant maintained* (GM) schools and *voluntary* schools. See *direct grant school*; *General Schools Budget (GSB)*; *governors*; *management*.

maintenance grant   A maintenance grant is awarded by a *local education authority* (LEA) for students' living costs when undertaking *degree*-level courses. See *grants*; *mandatory award*.

management   *Governors* have a general responsibility for the effective management of the school within the framework of national legislation and, in the case of *LEA*-maintained schools, LEA policies. Detailed decisions about the day-to-day running of the school are the responsibility of the head. The division of responsibilities in each school will be detailed in its articles of government but the head and governors should work in partnership. Schools are expected to review how the *curriculum* as a whole can best secure the overall aims of the 1988 Education Act and provide a satisfactory education for each pupil. Heads are expected to prepare *National Curriculum development plans*. LEAs determine the dates of school terms and holidays for county, controlled and maintained *special schools*, a duty discharged by the governors of aided, special agreement, *GM* schools and *CTCs*. Governors of schools determine the length of school sessions in the case of county, *voluntary controlled* and maintained special schools after consultation with the LEA. LEAs have a duty to arrange free *transport* where a pupil's circumstances make it necessary. Distance, safety and *special educational needs* are the most common criteria. See *accountability; Education Association (EA); Education Reform Act 1988; headteacher; instrument of government; local management of schools (LMS); school management team*.

mandatory award   These are the awards which *LEAs* must make to support eligible students taking first *degree* courses in *higher education*. The awards are means-tested. They cover the payment of fees to the *university* and maintenance of students during *term* time. The relative value of student *grants* has been declining over recent years. In 1991 the government introduced a student loan scheme. The intention is gradually to increase the value of the loan in relation to the student's overall level of support. See *designated course; maintenance grant*.

Manpower Services Commission (MSC)   The MSC was established in 1974, within the Department of Employment, as the national *training* agency. It introduced a series of schemes to engage more young people in training, for example the Training Opportunities Scheme (TOPS) and the *Youth Training Scheme* (YTS). It was replaced in 1988 by the Training Agency. See *industry; Technical and Vocational Education Initiative (TVEI); Training and Enterprise Councils (TECs)*.

mastery learning   This is the idea that with effective teaching over a suitable period of time mastery of any body or kind of *knowledge* is possible for any learner.

matching   This is the idea that any work set by a teacher should be matched to the *ability* and capability levels of the child. Some reports of schooling in England and Wales have suggested that there is a poor match between learning activities and pupils' needs. See *differentiated examinations; differentiation; pace*.

matriculation   The matriculation examination was set as a test for entrance to *university* but, since 1951, passes in two *A levels* have supplanted it. See *university entrance requirements*.

maturation   This is the idea that certain developments in children take place simply as a consequence of their growing older. It posits natural, innate development as a significant factor in intellectual and emotional development as well as planned or environmentally induced experiences. See *readiness*.

mature students   These are students who enter college or *university* later in life than most students. The definition of a mature student varies. In some institutions, and in respect of some courses, it may be over 21 but the most general definition of mature is over 25. Many institutions of *higher education* see part of their mission as broadening access to non-standard students, including students from ethnic minorities and students who left school before going on to *sixth form*. The *Open University* has been the pioneer of higher education provision for mature students, dispensing with traditional admissions criteria. Some mature students enrol on *access courses* which are designed as an introduction to, and preparation for, *degree*-level study. These are often offered by colleges of *further education*. See *adult education; continuing education*.

memory   Memory is the mental faculty through which experience is recorded and recalled. It is, therefore, an important factor in *learning*. Memory is sometimes sub-divided and described in terms of short-, medium- and long-term abilities to remember. See *rote learning; tables*.

mentor   A mentor is an adviser or friend within an educational context. In schools mentors are, increasingly, experienced teachers who take responsibility for tutoring student teachers when they are working on the school-based parts of their courses. A mentor might also be appointed to provide support for a newly appointed teacher in the *induction* year, or to support any new member of staff.

meritocracy   A meritocracy is based on the idea that education is provided for separate groups, each identified by talent or *ability*. In practice, talent or ability is often equated with scores from *intelligence* tests, an equation much derided in 1961 by Michael Young, who coined the term.

micro-teaching   This approach to initial teacher education was popular in the 1970s. The idea was to give student teachers practice in discrete elements of teaching, such as introducing a lesson, question and answer, explaining a *concept*, using visual aids or controlling a discussion, with a small group of children. The micro-teaching session was filmed and then the student would review his or her performance with a tutor. The intention was that increasingly sophisticated aspects of teaching would be developed in this way. Eventually the whole repertoire of teaching skills would be put together and practised in school experiences with full classes of children. See *teacher training*.

middle schools   These are schools which cater for the middle age range such as 8 to 12 or 9 to 13. Middle schools were first introduced in the early 1960s in some local authorities and by more in the post-*Plowden* period after 1967. The theory is that the middle years of schooling conform closely to a stage in most children's social and intellectual development. It was argued that transfer to *secondary school* at 11 cut into the child's stage of development in an unhelpful way. Middle schools attempted to combine the best aspects of the *primary* and secondary educational traditions. There was an emphasis on the generalist class teacher role lower down the school with more specialist teaching at the top of the age-range. Middle schools, however, tended to be classified as primary schools and received less funding per capita than they felt they required. In the post-1988 educational world there was a move away from the idea of middle schools, with a reversion to the more traditional primary–secondary break at age 11. See *age of transfer; first school; transition*.

Ministry of Education   Following the 1944 Education Act, the *Board of Education* was replaced by the Ministry of Education under a minister for Education. The Ministry was replaced by the *Department of Education and Science* in 1964. See *Butler Act (1944 Education Act)*.

mission statement   This is an expression of the mission, or strategic objectives, of an educational institution. It is a short statement which encapsulates the aspirations of the establishment. In an environment in which educational establishments increasingly adopt the concepts, language and rhetoric of the market place, the idea of an institutional mission has become a favourite. As schools adopt ideas like corporate *management*, management information systems, business plans, marketing policies, staff *appraisal* and *performance related pay*, the mission statement remains a potent symbol of the location of much educational management thinking in fashionable orthodoxies of the mid-1980s. See *information; school policy*.

mixed-ability group This is a teaching group which contains pupils representative of the range of *ability* in the school. Teaching in mixed-ability groups may be a way of describing organisational arrangements in a non-streamed school, where all *classes* have children of all ability levels, and it may also describe an organisational strategy within an individual classroom. Teaching in mixed-ability groups is common in primary schools. In secondary schools *banding*, *streaming*, or *setting* organisational arrangements are often used. See *comprehensive school*; *differentiated examinations*; *differentiation*; *matching*; *pace*.

mixed-age class This is a class made up of pupils from more than one age group. Such an arrangement is often found in small primary schools, where there may be insufficient pupil numbers to form single-age classes. Other terms used to describe mixed-age classes are *family* and *vertical grouping*. See *class*.

mock examination A mock examination is a trial run through an *examination* paper or process in anticipation of the real thing. Mocks or mock examinations are a traditional part of the school examination year, designed to give *GCSE* and *A level* candidates a dummy run which will help familiarise them with the examination process.

moderation This is the process of standardising agreements, such as *teacher's ratings*, to bring them into line with national *standards*. See *group moderation*.

modifications This term, and that of *disapplication*, refers to arrangements for lifting part, or all, of the *National Curriculum* requirement for individuals, schools or any other grouping specified by the Secretary of State. See *special educational needs (SEN)*.

module This is a definable section of work, of fixed length, with specific *objectives* and some form of terminal *assessment*. Modular courses are increasingly being introduced in the education system, particularly in *further* and *higher education*. Perceived advantages are that students can select individual pathways and that assessment is incremental and regular. A disadvantage perceived by some is the danger that too much flexibility may bring an incoherent student experience. The essence of a modular approach to course design is that discrete *curriculum* units are taught and assessed separately but form part of, or build into, a coherent whole. See *credit*; *foundation course*.

monitoring The idea of monitoring *performance* or *standards* is much in use. It refers to the idea of keeping a careful, regular check on various aspects of teaching and learning. It can be concerned with any aspects of the educational process such as numbers of applicants for a course, *admissions* procedures, student drop-out, *levels of attainment*, forms of *assessment* or approaches to teaching and learning.

Montessori schools Montessori schools are independent *nursery schools* which apply the methods developed by Maria Montessori in the late nineteenth century. There is much emphasis on natural expression in the Montessori method, and the idea of children learning through the senses. See *pre-school education*.

moral education The educational environment and certain planned educational experiences contribute to a child's moral development. In essence this refers to an individual's *behaviour*, his or her ability to treat other people well and to live in a community, and a child's ability to tell right from wrong. It is increasingly seen as a school's responsibility, as well as a parental obligation, to provide children with moral education. Part of this may be achieved through religious education syllabuses, but a school's contribution to a child's moral development will generally be planned in a more broadly-based way. See *counselling; guidance; pastoral care; personal and social education (PSE); sex education; spiritual, moral, social and cultural development; Sunday school*.

motivation A good deal of discussion about a child's progress in school is likely to centre on the extent of his or her motivation. Whatever explanations there may be for high or low motivation with regard to school work, highly motivated children are generally more likely to apply themselves to *learning* and to be successful in it. A distinction is frequently drawn between motivation which is externally imposed in some way, perhaps by the child's family or a teacher, and motivation which seems to spring from within the child, leading to a natural curiosity and drive to learn. The former kind is termed extrinsic and the latter is termed intrinsic motivation.

multicultural education Because we live in a society which includes many different cultures, including those of *ethnic minorities*, it is felt that there should be a multicultural basis to the education we provide. This entails consideration of a school's formal and informal curriculum, so that a school's policies value cultural diversity, draw on a range of cultural contexts, give children of all cultural backgrounds positive role models and develop appropriate practice with regard to worship and religious education. Devising appropriate educational responses to multicultural society in ways which satisfy the expectations of all groups is difficult to achieve, and sometimes arouses controversy. See *race; school policy*.

multidisciplinary   See *interdisciplinary*.

multilateral education   This is a precursor of the idea of the *comprehensive school*. The idea of a multilateral school was to place the three post-1944 types of education – *grammar, secondary modern* and *technical* – on the same site. Thus the three types would have coexisted side by side. Unlike the comprehensive school, they followed distinct and separate educational programmes. See *Butler Act (1944 Education Act)*.

multiple choice test   This is a form of objective *assessment* in which candidates are presented with a series of possible responses to a given question. Candidates normally indicate which response they prefer by a tick. The tests are quick to administer and reliable. See *objective test; testing*.

Munn Report   This was an influential report on the education of third- and fourth-year *secondary* pupils in Scotland. It was chaired by Sir James Munn and published in 1977. It was a significant report which emphasised the distinctiveness of Scotland's approach to educational provision, a distinctiveness which was accentuated as England and Wales adopted the statutory *National Curriculum*. See *Scotland: Five to Fourteen Development Programme*.

museums   Museum education has become increasingly well-developed and professional. Many local and national museums have established good education services, usually with a designated museum education officer. Much good work has been done including explanatory notes on collections, availability of personnel to talk to children about collections and development of loan collections for use in schools. There is some evidence that the specificity of the *National Curriculum* in history encouraged museums to review practice and align their services more directly to schools' needs. See *school visit*.

~ N ~

National Anti-Racist Movement in Education (NAME) This association counters racism in education and fosters anti-racism at all levels of the system. See *race*. For more information contact:

> National Anti-Racist Movement in Education
> PO Box 9
> Walsall
> West Midlands
> WS1 3SF
>
> Telephone No: 0161 442 2673

National Association for Education in Art and Design The objectives of the Association are to further art, *craft and design* education and the professional interests of those engaged in it. For further information contact:

> National Association for Education in Art and Design
> 7a High Street
> Corsham
> Wiltshire
> SN13 0ES
>
> Telephone No: 01249 714825

National Association for Gifted Children (NAGC) This organisation, established in 1966, represents and promotes the educational needs of gifted children. See *gifted children*. For further information contact:

National Association for Gifted Children
Park Campus
Boughton Green Road
Northampton
NN2 7AL

Telephone No: 01604 792300

National Association for Governors and Managers (NAGM)
This is a group representing parents and teachers which from 1970 campaigned for changes in the way governing bodies were constituted. In the wake of the changes in the composition and responsibilities of governing bodies introduced in the 1981, 1986 and 1988 Education Acts, the NAGM has acted as an influential association representing *governors'* interests. NAGM runs a free advice line for governors and publishes a series of information sheets on all aspects of governors' work. For further information contact:

National Association for Governors and Managers (NAGM)
Suite 36/38
21 Bennett's Hill
Birmingham
B2 5QP

Telephone No: 0121 643 5787

National Association of Headteachers (NAHT)   The principal association for *headteachers* and *deputy headteachers*. See *unions*.

National Association for Primary Education (NAPE)   NAPE is an organisation of parents, teachers, school governors and others interested in the education of children from birth to 13. It has a central headquarters and local branches. As well as local events, it organises a national conference, publishes a journal and engages in lobbying for the cause of *primary* education. See *Home and School Council*. For further information contact:

National Association for Primary Education (NAPE)
National Office, Queen's Building
University of Leicester
Barrack Road
Northampton
NN2 6AF

Telephone No: 01604 36326

National Association of Schoolmasters/Union of Women Teachers (NAS/UWT)   The two separate unions merged in 1976 to form the second largest teachers' union after the *National Union of Teachers*. See *unions*.

National Association for Staff Development (NASD)   This is an association for all interested in promoting, managing, researching, organising and evaluating *staff development*. The association organises meetings and conferences, and disseminates information. It issues a newsletter. For further information contact:

> National Association for Staff Development
> 30 St Helena Road
> Colchester
> CO3 3BA
>
> Telephone No: 01206 571258

National Association of Teachers in Further and Higher Education (NATFHE)   This association of lecturers working in *further* and *higher education* was formed in 1975 when the Association of Teachers in Technical Institutions (ATTI) merged with the Association of Teachers in Colleges and Departments of Education (ATCDE). Since the incorporation of the polytechnics into the new *university* system, NATFHE has formed a University and College Lecturers' Union (UCLU). For further information contact:

> NATFHE
> 27 Britannia Street
> London
> WC1X 9JP
>
> Telephone No: 0171 837 3936

National Association for the Teaching of English (NATE)
This is the foremost professional subject group for teachers of English. Membership is drawn from *primary* and *secondary schools*. NATE holds a national conference, although most of its events are local. It emerged as a significant professional influence in the debate about the shape of the *National Curriculum* in English and in disputes about appropriate arrangements for *assessment* and *testing*. For further information contact:

National Association for the Teaching of English (NATE)
50 Broadfield Road
Broadfield Business Centre
Sheffield
S8 0XJ

Telephone No: 01742 555419

National Audio-Visual Aids Library The library has a comprehensive range of holdings relevant to audio-visual and video support to education and training. For further information contact:

National Audio-Visual Aids Library
7 Paxton Place
London
SE7

Telephone No: 0181 670 4247

National Children's Bureau (NCB) The Bureau exists to develop awareness and promote research about children and young people. It has a wide membership including higher education institutions, health and social service organisations and individuals with a concern for young people. The Bureau conducted a well-known longitudinal study of children born in one week in 1958, reporting findings about the children at certain stages in their lives. For further information contact:

National Children's Bureau
8 Wakley Street
London
EC1V 7QE

Telephone No: 0171 278 9441

National Commission on Education The National Commission was established following a presidential speech by Sir Claus Moser to the *British Association for the Advancement of Science* in 1991. It followed the refusal of the government to set up a Royal Commission on the condition of education in England and Wales. The National Commission was funded by the Paul Hamlyn Foundation and went about its business in the manner of a Royal Commission. It made a series of proposals about education, from *nursery school* to the *university* and beyond, in its report, 'Learning to Succeed', which was issued in 1994. For further information contact:

National Commission on Education
344–354 Gray's Inn Road
London
WC1X 8BP

Telephone No: 0171 278 4411

National Confederation of Parent–Teacher Associations (NCPTA) This influential association of *Parent–Teacher Associations* (PTAs) gives advice and support for members and others on home–school issues. It can also provide information on local associations. See *Home and School Council; home–school relations; pressure group*. For further information contact:

National Confederation of Parent–Teacher Associations (NCPTA)
2 Ebbsfleet Industrial Estate
Gravesend
Kent
DA11 9D2

Telephone No: 01474 560618

National Council for Educational Technology (NCET) The purpose of the Council is to extend the role of educational *technology* in schools. For further information contact:

National Council for Educational Technology
Sir William Lyons Road
University of Warwick
Science Park
Coventry
CV4 7E2

Telephone No: 01203 416994

National Council for Vocational Qualifications (NCVQ) The purpose of the Council is to develop a coherent system of vocational qualifications. It is the NCVQ which has drawn up the national framework of *National Vocational Qualifications* (NVQs). The framework is made up of four levels, depending on the complexity of vocational skills involved in particular occupations. See *vocational education*. For further information contact:

National Council for Vocational Qualifications
222 Euston Road
London
NW1 2BZ

Telephone No: 0171 387 9898

National Curriculum   The National Curriculum is the compulsory *curriculum* laid down by the government for all pupils in *state schools* during the period of compulsory schooling (ages 5 to 16). It includes the *core* and *foundation subjects* and their associated *attainment targets, programmes of study* and *assessment* arrangements.

The work in National Curriculum subjects is arranged in programmes of study for four *Key Stages* (Year 1 to 2; Year 3 to 6; Year 7 to 9; Year 10 to 11).

The basic curriculum consists of the National Curriculum and religious education (RE). The National Curriculum is made up of three *core subjects* (English, mathematics and science) and seven other *foundation subjects* (history, geography, technology and physical education in all Key Stages; music and art in Key Stages 1, 2 and 3 and a modern foreign language in Key Stages 3 and 4). Pupils at Key Stage 4 who study the full course in history are excepted from the study of geography and vice versa.

The National Curriculum in a particular subject does not apply to pupils where the majority of the class have taken a *General Certificate of Secondary Education* (GCSE) or equivalent examination in the subject at least one year before they reached the end of Key Stage 4.

Pupils in the 1992–3 cohort for Key Stage 4 who are following courses in physics, chemistry and biology leading to GCSE are exempt from the National Curriculum in science.

The 1994 Review of the National Curriculum by Sir Ron *Dearing* proposed a simplification and reduction of the statutory requirements. These changes will be implemented from August 1995 for pupils aged five to 14 and from August 1996 for 14- to 16-year-olds. See *combined course; continuity and progression; cross-curricular; curriculum guidelines; disapplication; Education Reform Act 1988; end of key stage statements (EKSS); full course; Grants for Education Support and Training (GEST); levels of attainment; modifications; National Curriculum Council; non-statutory examples; non-statutory guidance; profile component (PC); Scotland: Five to Fourteen Development Programme; short course; standard assessment tasks (SATs); statements of attainment (SOA); statutory order; strand; Task Group on Assessment and Testing (TGAT).*

National Curriculum Council (NCC)   The National Curriculum Council was established in 1988 under the *Education Reform Act*. Its purpose was to work on detailed proposals for each subject and to offer advice on the implementation of the *National Curriculum*. Its first chairman was Duncan Graham. In 1993 the NCC merged with the *Schools Examination and Assessment Council* (SEAC) to form the *School Curriculum and Assessment Authority* (SCAA). See *curriculum guidelines; levels of attainment; non-statutory guidance; whole curriculum*.

National Extension College (NEC)   The purpose of the College is to provide educational opportunities for adults who do not continue with their studies after compulsory schooling. The NEC is independent and operates through the use of correspondence courses. See *adult education; distance learning; open learning*. For further information contact:

> National Extension College
> 18 Brooklands Avenue
> Cambridge
> CB2 2HN
>
> Telephone No: 01223 316644

National Foundation for Educational Research (NFER)   The NFER is the foremost and best-known educational research unit in the United Kingdom. It was founded in 1946 by the *local education authorities*. It is independent of government, raising funds from subscription and research commissions. It employs a staff of full-time researchers. It has a formidable record of publication. For further information contact:

> National Foundation for Educational Research
> The Mere
> Upton Park
> Slough
> Berks
> SL1 2DQ
>
> Telephone No: 01753 74123

National Institute of Adult Continuing Education (NIACE)
The Institute is concerned with the provision of opportunities for *continuing education* for adults. It draws funds from *local education authorities* and government. As the foremost national centre in its field it acts

as a coordination and information centre. Under its umbrella is the Adult Literacy and Basic Skills Unit (ALBSU). See *adult education; adult literacy*. For further information contact:

> National Institute of Adult Continuing Education (NIACE)
> 19B De Montfort Street
> Leicester
> LE1 7GE
>
> Telephone No: 01533 551451

National Nursery Examination Board (NNEB)   The NNEB is the examinations and validation body for qualifications for *nursery nurses*. Most NNEB courses are taken in colleges of further education with supervision of practice in a nursery. In order to obtain the Diploma in Nursery Nursing students generally undertake two years' full-time study. For more information contact:

> National Nursery Examination Board (NNEB)
> 8 Chequer Street
> St Albans
> Herts
> AL1 3XZ
>
> Telephone No: 01727 867609

National Record of Achievement (NRA)   This is a scheme for recording pupils' achievements at the end of schooling. Various schemes were developed locally in the 1970s and 1980s. The NRA scheme became compulsory in 1993. See *record of achievement*.

National Union of Students (NUS)   The organisation acts as a coordinating national body for local *student unions*. There is a full-time executive. The NUS organises a national conference and campaigns on student-related matters such as student *grants* and loans. The NUS has become involved in the discussion of students' rights and entitlements in *higher education*, issuing a widely praised Students' Charter in 1993. The government's proposals to limit the powers of student unions, set out in the 1994 Education Bill, were withdrawn following opposition in the House of Lords. For further information contact:

National Union of Students
461 Holloway Road
London
N7 6LJ

Telephone No: 0171 272 8900

National Union of Teachers (NUT)   The principal association for teachers, drawing its strength predominantly from membership in primary schools. See *unions*.

National Vocational Qualifications (NVQ)   A national system for vocational qualifications has been established by the *National Council for Vocational Qualifications* (NCVQ). The framework, developed since 1986, seeks to express work-place skills in a series of five levels:

Level 1:   *Competence* in a range of work activities;
Level 2:   Competence in more complex activities;
Level 3:   Competence in a broad range of activities including supervisory work;
Level 4:   Complex technical or professional work;
Level 5:   Competence equivalent to that of a *postgraduate* vocational qualification.

General National Vocational Qualifications (GNVQ), introduced in 1992, are seen as a competence-based approach to post-16 education. The idea is to provide *training* which combines job-specific competences with general preparation in five subject areas relating to a range of vocations. The GNVQ programme is generally one year full-time. See *Certificate of Pre-Vocational Education (CPVE); practical assessment; Royal Society of Arts (RSA); vocational education*. For further information contact:

National Council for Vocational Qualifications and Vocational Education
222 Euston Road
London
NW1 2BZ

Telephone No: 0171 387 9898

National Youth Agency   The Agency provides information for those involved in the education of young people on the management and training of youth workers and for policy makers. This is a government-funded body. For further information contact:

National Youth Agency
17–23 Albion Street
Leicester
LE1 6GD

Telephone No: 01533 471200

neighbourhood school The idea that a school should predominantly draw its pupils from its local *catchment area* captures the idea of a neighbourhood school. A contrast would be a *selective school* to which pupils travelled from a variety of locations. The term is more often used in the United States than in the United Kingdom. See *admission*; *non-selective schools*; *open enrolment*.

New Education Fellowship (NEF) The Fellowship was founded in 1921 to support *progressivism* in education. It changed its name to the World Education Fellowship in 1966.

newly qualified teachers (NQT) See *probationary year*.

non-contact time This is time when teachers are not teaching classes of children. It is time when teachers can plan or mark work, or undertake other responsibilities assigned by the headteacher. There is generally felt to be a need to provide teachers with more non-contact time, especially in primary schools, where direct teaching takes practically all a teacher's time. See *contact ratio*; *free periods*; *teacher–class ratio*.

non-selective schools A non-selective school is one which operates a policy of *open enrolment* and does not select pupils according to their intelligence level, religion and cultural background or parental income. See *bipartite system*; *comprehensive school*; *selective schools*.

non-statutory examples Within each *statutory order*, in each subject of the *National Curriculum*, points could be illustrated by non-statutory examples. They were generally printed in italics, to show that they had no statutory force. The examples could pertain to *statements of attainment*, *end of key stage statements* or aspects of the *programme of study*.

non-statutory guidance (NSG) This was guidance produced by the *National Curriculum Council* (NCC) to accompany the *statutory order* for each subject. The NSG was designed to fit in the ring binder with the order, but it had no statutory force. In sum NSG was intended to help teachers by giving illustrations and ideas for activities or organisation of children in each subject area. The *Dearing Report*, attempting to reduce the amount of paperwork circulated to schools, proposed an end to NSG.

norm-referenced testing Norm-referenced testing is the term used to describe a process in which *testing* procedures are designed to produce a set of results which places students in positions related to the normal curve of distribution. In such an arrangement a few people will score particularly well or particularly badly, while the vast majority will perform somewhere in-between. The procedure is contrasted with *criterion-referenced testing* in which students' performances are simply tested against criteria of *competence* or understanding. There is no expectation of distributing results in a certain way, by comparing one student's performance with another. Rather, under criterion-referenced testing it would be possible for 100 per cent of the students to achieve a mark of 100 per cent. See *assessment; grades*.

Nuffield Science Funded by the Nuffield Foundation, projects to improve science teaching and science curricula were initiated in the 1960s. The projects were chiefly aimed at *secondary schools* and new *O* and *A level* syllabuses were designed.

numeracy This is the idea that all educated people should be numerate, in other words able to manipulate numbers, understand numerical relationships and have insight into numerical processes. Our society has perhaps given more emphasis to virtues of *literacy*, a tradition thought by some to bedevil British education. See *basic skills; oracy*.

nursery class This is a group of nursery children, and/or their accommodation, usually within the *infant* or *primary school* building. A nursery unit normally comprises separate accommodation built or adapted for nursery-age children. See *pre-school education*.

nursery nurse This is a two-year-trained assistant who works with young children. The awarding body is the *National Nursery Examination Board* (NNEB).

nursery school Nursery schools provide *pre-school education* for children from the age of two to five. They may be independent or provided by the state. See *childminders; day nurseries; kindergarten;*

Montessori schools; playgroups; pre-school playgroup (PPG). For further information contact:

British Association for Early Childhood Education (BAECE)
111 City View House
463 Bethnal Green Road
London
E2 9QH

Telephone No: 0171 739 7594

National Children's Bureau
Under Fives Unit
8 Wakley Street
London
EC1V 7QE

Telephone No: 0171 278 9441

O level The O level examination is the *General Certificate of Education* (GCE) ordinary level examination. It was intended for the brightest *secondary* pupils up to the age of 16, and in the main was originally limited to those intending to go on to *higher education* and the professions. In 1965 the *Certificate of Secondary Education* (CSE) was introduced for less bright pupils at 16. In general a CSE grade 1 was regarded as equivalent to a grade C at O level. In 1988 the two examinations were brought together in the *General Certificate of Secondary Education* (GCSE), a common leaving examination for pupils of all abilities. Such an examination was seen by many as a logical consequence of a *comprehensive* secondary school system with substantial elements of a common secondary curriculum. See *School Certificate*.

objective test This is a form of *testing* which leaves no room for teacher judgement. Often taking the form of *multiple choice* questionnaire-type papers, or questions demanding one-word answers, the pupil is either right or wrong, or at any rate responses are compared with a very limited number of permitted responses. With increased emphasis on the time which can be given over to testing in all sectors of education, the attractions of objective testing are clearly those of speed and efficiency. Such an approach normally needs to be put alongside additional forms of *examining* so that a more rounded view of the pupil's *learning* is secured.

objectives This term relates to the intentions of teaching and *learning*. Objectives are a means by which teachers can specify the outcomes they expect to result from *instruction*. Objectives are generally regarded as more specific than educational aims, although objectives themselves may be specified with greater or lesser precision. An aim of teaching history, for example, might be to inculcate in pupils a sense of enjoyment in exploring old buildings, whereas an objective for a particular visit would indicate the kind of observation, recording and comparisons which might be undertaken. In other words, objectives are statements in terms of *knowledge, skills* and *attitudes* of desired educational outcomes. An influential idea of American origin was that of curriculum planning by *behavioural objectives*. This was the idea that all learning outcomes should be predicted in terms of observable changes of behaviour in pupils. The specification of these learning objectives became very popular in some quarters, leading to intricate constructions of learning taxonomies, classified into various domains. For others such an approach appeared burdensome and mechanistic, attempting to invest an exploratory educative process with too much certainty.

Office of Her Majesty's Chief Inspector of Schools (OHMCI)

The Office of Her Majesty's Chief Inspector of Schools for England (OHMCI) is a non-ministerial government department which regulates the system of inspection introduced under the 1992 Further and Higher Education Act. The Office's more familiar title is *OFSTED* (Office for Standards in Education). Her Majesty's Chief Inspector of Schools (HMCI) is responsible for the registration of *inspectors* and the arrangements for the inspection of schools, apart from the inspection of religious education in those voluntary and GM schools where it is not legally required to be provided in accordance with an agreed syllabus. In these cases responsibility for the inspection of denominational education falls to the school governors (Sections 9, 10 and 13 of the 1992 Act). See *Her Majesty's Inspectorate; inspection team member; registered inspector*. For further information contact:

OHMCI
Elizabeth House
York Road
London
SE1 7PH

Telephone No: 0171 421 6800

Office for Standards in Education (OFSTED)

There was a good deal of surprise when the government began to convert the long-established schools inspectorate into OFSTED. *Her Majesty's Inspectors* (HMIs) had been a respected part of the quality assurance system at a national level since the nineteenth century and they were influential as the eyes and ears of the minister out in the country. But in 1992 the number of HMIs was reduced and OFSTED took its place alongside OFWAT, OFGAS and OFTEL as just another public utility inspection agency. OFSTED became responsible for the new cycle of school inspections, where all schools were to be inspected every four years, and for training a new cadre of independent *inspectors*. The new, privatised approach to inspection organised by OFSTED put all inspection work out to tender on a commercial basis. See *quality*. For further information contact:

OFSTED
Elizabeth House
York Road
London
SE1 7PH

Telephone No: 0171 421 6800

ombudsman   The ombudsman is appointed to investigate complaints, including complaints about the education service. For further information contact:

Commission for Local Administration in England
21 Queen Anne's Gate
London
SW1H 9BU

Telephone No: 0171 915 3210

open admission   This is a policy of allowing open entry to courses without requiring pre-specified entry qualifications. This is the way in which the *Open University*, for example, operates its admissions policy so that adults are attracted to study in higher education. See *access course; adult education; continuing education; distance learning; mature students; university entrance requirements*.

Open College   The idea of the Open College, set up by the *Department for Trade and Industry* in 1987, was to give a training push to British employers. In effect the Open College was a marketing operation, offering sponsored training through contact points in local further education colleges. See *vocational education*. For more information contact:

The Open College
781 Wilmslow Road
Didsbury
Manchester
M20 8RW

Telephone No: 0161 434 0007

Open College of the Arts   The idea of the College is to open *distance learning* opportunities for adults. It is modelled on the success of the *Open University*. Some courses involve opportunity for local support groups and supervision. See *adult education; continuing education; open learning*. For further information contact:

The Open College of the Arts
Freepost
Barnsley
South Yorkshire
S70 6BR

Telephone No: 01226 730495

open day   This is the day when an educational institution is open for visits from members of the public. Open days are seen as a valuable way of informing the local community, and prospective customers, of the quality and range of work undertaken. They are sometimes organised in such a way that members of staff are available for consultation and to give advice.

open enrolment   A significant aspect of the government's educational reform programme in the 1980s was the idea of providing more parental choice. One facet of this was the policy of open enrolment. The principle is that *parents* choose the school they wish their children to attend and are not limited in exercising that choice by the rules, regulations and management of *local education authorities*. There are clearly problems with the policy of open enrolment when more parents wish to choose that school than there are places available. When that happens LEAs operate rules, which broadly favour the application of pupils from within the school's *catchment area*. It is possible for parents to appeal against LEA decisions. See *admission; Education Reform Act 1988; non-selective schools; Parents' Charter; selective schools*.

open evening   This is the opportunity for *parents* to visit school to discuss their children's progress with teachers. They are usually held once a year. There is often an opportunity to see samples of children's work, especially in the *primary school*. In primary schools parents would normally speak to the child's *class* teacher and the *headteacher* if a particular concern has been raised. In *secondary schools* there are more subject teachers to see, as well as the child's *form* teacher. See *home–school relations*; *parents' evening*.

open learning   This is a form of learning which is open to all, does not require pre-admission qualifications and does not involve attendance at an educational institution. In effect, open learning is learning which takes place at home, normally with the support of centrally produced learning materials, as in a *correspondence course*. Learning may be supported by *IT*, video or audio materials. Course assignments are marked by a *tutor* who the student may or may not meet depending on the particular open learning arrangements in force. Some open learning systems provide opportunities for support meetings at local centres. The most widely known and successful form of open learning is that provided by the *Open University*. See *adult education; continuing education; distance learning; educational television; National Extension College (NEC); Open College of the Arts*.

open-plan schools   Open-plan schools became fashionable in the 1960s and are often associated with *progressive primary* education. In open-plan schools the traditional structure of the individual, enclosed classroom staffed by a single teacher responsible for the whole curriculum is abandoned. In its place an open-plan arrangement has larger working spaces in which there is opportunity for more flexibility in grouping children, use of space and deployment of staff. No one model of open-plan schools exists and many forms were developed. The openness of open-plan schools, and the more flexible opportunities they apparently offered, were regarded by some as representative of a new style of primary education. More critical voices looked at some practical consequences, such as the need for elaborate planning if open-plan teaching was to work well and problems in keeping on top of assessment. See *teaching methods*; *teaching style*.

Open University   One of the great success stories of twentieth-century educational development, the Open University (OU) was founded in 1966. The idea of the University was to offer a second chance to adults who had not continued their studies beyond compulsory schooling for whatever reason. There are no restricting admissions criteria to OU courses and that sense of openness remains. Students are offered a range of study materials and use is also made of TV and radio broadcasts. Attendance for support at local centres and on summer schools are part of the OU approach. Courses of study are wide, embracing short courses, aspects of professional and individual development to supervision of doctorates. See *adult education;*

continuing education; distance learning; educational television; mature students; open admission; Open College of the Arts; open learning; prison education; reader. For further information contact:

> The Open University
> Walton Hall
> Milton Keynes
> Buckinghamshire
> MK7 6AA
>
> Telephone No: 01908 274066

opting out   This term refers to the decision of a school to opt out of local authority control and secure *independent* or *grant maintained status* (GMS). This provision was enshrined in the 1988 *Education Reform Act*, a significant part of the policy of diminishing the influence of *LEAs* and encouraging schools to become autonomous, competing mini-businesses.

options   The idea of subjects in *secondary school* being optional at some point is long-established. In effect all pupils take a core of subjects, normally, English, mathematics and science, through to 16 and select certain options at the age of 14 when they begin the *GCSE*. The system was criticised on the grounds that pupils sometimes made poor choices, or were given inadequate advice, in such a way as to limit their subsequent opportunities. One consequence of the introduction of the *National Curriculum* might have been the introduction of a common secondary school *curriculum* for all pupils up to the age of 16. However, option systems still operate and children choose the range of GCSEs they will study at the age of 14.

ORACLE   The acronym stands for Observational Research and Classroom Learning Evaluation. The project, based at the School of Education, University of Leicester, was concerned with the relationship between *primary* pupils' progress and behaviour, and the different *teaching styles* practised by their teachers. One of the important conclusions was that teaching style significantly affected pupils' progress and *attainment*. It was operational between 1975 and 1980.

Ordinary National Certificate (ONC)   This *vocational* qualification, awarded after a part-time course of two years, was restricted to a narrow band of subjects and, broadly speaking, was equated to *A levels*. ONC was phased out when the *Business and Technology*

Education Council (BTEC) introduced appropriate certificates. The *National Council for Vocational Qualifications* is now responsible for the qualification.

Ordinary National Diploma (OND) Like *ONC,* Ordinary National Diploma (OND) is a *vocational* qualification usually awarded after two years of part-time study – or sandwich course. OND was phased out when the *Business and Technology Education Council* (BTEC) introduced an appropriate replacement. The *National Council for Vocational Qualifications* is now responsible for the qualification.

oracy The term focuses on ability to speak. It was brought to prominence as a key objective for schooling alongside *literacy* and *numeracy.* The ability to communicate is clearly an important skill for life and work. Speaking and listening feature as explicit parts of the *National Curriculum* in English, but are clearly relevant to all subjects. See *basic skills.*

oral An oral examination is a normal part of *GCSE* examinations in modern languages and music. The oral examination tests pupils' ability to understand a language and to speak clearly. The normal form of an oral examination is a conversation on a given topic. The oral examination is a familiar form of *assessment* in higher education. Known as the *viva* voce, the oral examination is used as part of the process of examining higher degrees including the PhD. An examiner in this situation quizzes the examinee on the basis of what he or she has written.

outreach The outreach approach is proactive; teachers or lecturers make a point of bringing courses and activities into the community. The aim is to introduce young people to education courses and, in the long term, to encourage them to continue studying at further or higher levels.

Oxbridge A short-hand term to denote the universities of Oxford and Cambridge. See *collegiate university; degrees.*

~ P ~

pace   Pace is an important element in lesson planning; teachers have to consider pupils' *abilities, motivation* and attention span when judging the order, presentation and speed at which *knowledge* can be acquired. See *differentiation; matching; mixed-ability group*.

paired reading   The idea lying behind paired reading is that children will learn well when they work closely with another child at certain stages in learning to read. See *reading*.

parent governors   It is a requirement that parents of children attending a school are represented on the governing body. The proposal originated in a recommendation of the 1977 Taylor Report and was part of the 1981 Education Act. Parent governors make up one quarter of a school's governing body. They are elected by secret ballot for a period of four years. See *governors*.

Parent–Teacher Association (PTA)   It is not a statutory responsibility for all schools to establish PTAs but most do. They are voluntary organisations of school staff and parents which aim to support the school in a variety of ways. They bring parents and teachers together in one organisation for educational, social and, increasingly, fundraising purposes. See *home–school relations; National Confederation of Parent–Teacher Associations (NCPTA)*.

parents   Part of the purpose of the 1988 *Education Reform Act* is to involve parents more closely in the education of their children. The intention is that parents should exercise more choice about the schools their children attend by having more *information* about a school's performance. The principal source of information is the publication of *league tables* of test and examination results. Parents will become more involved in the governance of schools through representation on schools' governing bodies, leading to more local *accountability*. A ballot of parents is the key part of arrangements to establish a grant maintained school outside local authority control. Parents may also contribute to the work of a school through a *Parent–Teacher Association* (PTA). In practice the extension of parental choice, for example in respect of selection of schools, has been controversial and a bone of political contention. See *home–school relations; open evening; parents' evening; reports.*

Parents' Charter The Parents' Charter is one of the initiatives developed by the government as part of its Citizens' Charter. The Charter, announced in 1991, is contained in the booklet 'The Parents' Charter: You and Your Child's Education'. It is designed to improve parents' access to the *information* they require about their children's education so that schools become more accountable and parents are able to make better-informed choices. The Parents' Charter, then, is a part of the government's drive to raise *standards* in education by more closely involving parents in decisions about their children's education.

The Parents' Charter requires schools to publish test and examination results and their *truancy* rates. It include plans for annual reports on children's progress. Under proposals for the inspection of schools, all schools now have full inspections every four years and are required to communicate the results to parents. LEAs are required to compile comparative data on schools in their area. The early experience of publishing results of examinations and truancy demonstrated the problem of ensuring that all schools applied the criteria and guidelines consistently. There was evidence that some schools boosted their examination success rates by only entering as official candidates those pupils they confidently expected to pass. In respect of truancy it was clear that the status of the terms 'authorised' and 'unauthorised' absence initially caused considerable difficulty.

Critics of the various Citizen Charter initiatives argue that they constitute little more than an expensive public relations exercise, giving parents the illusion of choice where little real choice exists for most parents and masking a failure by central government to devote sufficient resources to education. See *accountability; league tables; prospectus; records.*

parents' evening It has become general practice to hold *open evenings* for parents to visit schools in order to discuss the progress of their children with teachers. In primary schools it is common for samples of children's work to be available for parents to see. Some schools organise open evenings for parents and there is a focus on explaining the school's approach to teaching a particular subject. Such evenings might concern themselves with investigative approaches in science teaching and problem-solving in mathematics in the primary school, for example. See *home–school relations*.

participant observation   This refers to collecting data in the field, when the researcher may decide to participate in the activities of the group being observed, without revealing his or her own identity, and record the actions and behaviour of its members.

partnership teaching   This is a form of teaching commonly used to meet the language learning needs of *bilingual pupils*. It is used as a criterion in the allocation of grants to support language teaching for these pupils under the Home Office's *Section 11* grants. Under partnership teaching, the class teacher and *language support teacher* together plan and teach a programme of in-class language learning. See *bilingual assistants*.

part-time education   This describes a form of education pursued by students, normally adult students, alongside work or family responsibilities. Most students in school are there full-time, although there have been times, for example when teachers have taken industrial action, when schooling has become part-time for some. See *full-time equivalence*.

part-time (PT) teacher   This is a term used to indicate that individual teaching posts or members of staff are part-time. It is possible that more use is being made of part-time teaching staff and staff on fixed-term rather than permanent contracts as schools take responsibility for managing their own budgets under local management of schools (LMS). See *full-time equivalence*.

pass mark   This is the mark set by examiners as the point in the mark-scale below which the result is failure. See *borderline; cut-off point*.

pass rate   The number of candidates who pass an *examination* or *test* may be expressed as a percentage or ratio in order to establish the pass rate. See *league tables*.

passive learning   This kind of learning is usually associated with *transmission teaching*; pupils are expected to absorb *knowledge* in a passive, mechanistic way. Since no opportunities to participate are allowed for, the learner's level of involvement is extremely low. See *active learning; rote learning; teaching style*.

pastoral care   This refers to those parts of a school's systems and structures which are designed to promote and support the general welfare of pupils. In a secondary school, pastoral care is likely to be the principal concern of a form *tutor* supported by a head of year. A *deputy head* in a large school will commonly have oversight of, and managerial responsibility for, pastoral care. An aspect of this care may be access to staff with expertise in *guidance* and *counselling*. In primary schools, the class teacher is generally seen as having responsibility for all aspects of a child's academic and social development in school, including their *attendance* and *behaviour*. In general, there is less likelihood of the management structure of primary schools dividing its functions so as to concentrate on either the academic or the pastoral. See *house system; moral education; personal and social education (PSE); spiritual, moral, social and cultural development*.

payment by results   Under the revised code introduced in 1863, funding for schools became dependent on the outcomes of yearly examinations of pupils by *Her Majesty's Inspectorate* (HMI) and on required levels of minimal attendance. This system of payment by results was retained for about forty years and, from time to time, the principles underlying it have been discussed under different guises. See *performance related pay*.

pedagogy   This term is little used in Britain but quite widely used overseas. In essence it means a science of teaching, one concerned with the interrelationship of *teaching method* and *curriculum*. The term psycho-pedagogy develops the idea of pedagogy further by basing it more firmly on psychological principles about learning and teaching.

performance indicators (PIs)   These are measures of effective performance, often statistical, which were increasingly applied to the performance of educational institutions in the 1980s. They are usually measures of output, for example course completion rates, examination success rates or the proportion of school leavers moving to higher education or employment. They might also deal with *attendance* rates in a school, and *truancy*, or attempt to measure value for money by comparing spending per pupil in different schools, or the numbers of teachers employed. PIs are criticised by some for their main concentration on educational products rather than processes, for applying industrial measures to an educational service, for confusing efficiency with effectiveness and for drawing attention away from the particular setting of an individual school. For example, one school might perform poorly in comparison with another in a more favoured location, yet its *value added* performance might be superior. It is claimed that excessive concentration on statistical measures of performance can lead to too little emphasis on the quality of teaching and learning. The contrary view holds that PIs are a useful contribution to judging schools, that they should be used alongside other evidence, that schools should be expected to give value for money and that PIs are a significant contribution to the assessment of management competence. See *accountability*; *league tables*; *pupil–teacher ratio*.

performance related pay (PRP)   PRP is a system of rewarding individuals for the excellence of their work. Its application to education has been controversial, although it is increasingly being introduced as an element of pay schemes in higher education. A proportion of a manager's pay might be set against such work targets as the achievement of efficiencies, development of new courses, the attraction of funding or the achievement of admission targets. The government has been anxious to establish a PRP culture in education and in the 1992–3 pay settlement required HE institutions to develop PRP schemes for their staff. The application of PRP to the work of individual teachers is likely to stimulate controversy. There is some research evidence, mainly American, which indicates that such schemes can be ineffective, leading to divisiveness and a breaking down of that sense of shared responsibility which characterises the performance of the most effective educational institutions. It is also notoriously difficult to establish criteria which allow for fair comparison of the work of individual teachers in different settings. See *appraisal*; *payment by results*; *performance indicators*.

performance test   In a performance test, candidates are tested on performance skills, e.g. dancing, singing, gymnastics. In another context, a pupil may be examined, by performance test, on his or her *attainment*.

peripatetic teacher   This is a teacher who works in a number of schools, usually offering specialist teaching in an area where individual schools would be unable to employ such a teacher. Many peripatetic teachers are teachers of music, giving pupils instruction in playing musical instruments. Peripatetic music teachers are employed by LEAs who take responsibility for managing this inter-school service. Under LMS schools are less inclined to pay the costly expense of individual music tuition. Peripatetic teachers are used by some LEAs to provide support for children with *special educational needs*. The posts of many peripatetic teachers have been lost as LEAs have reduced the range of services for which they can take responsibility. Peripatetic help can also be provided at home in certain circumstances, for example when children have been involved in an accident or are incapacitated for some other reason such as disability. See *learning support*; *support teachers*.

personal and social education (PSE)   PSE is generally offered in secondary schools, usually in Years 9, 10 and 11. It deals with pupils' personal and social development and is one of the ways in which schools seek to promote pupils' *spiritual and moral development*. PSE often takes place in pupils' registration or form groups, introducing opportunities to discuss such topics as *health education*, political education and aspects of social relationships including *sex education*. The purpose of PSE is to help educate pupils for life outside and following school. In primary schools this area of education is generally not specifically identified on the timetable. Instead, it tends to be seen as permeating all parts of the curriculum in *cross-curricular* elements. The *National Curriculum Council* recognised the importance of PSE, identified it as a cross-curricular theme and published a book giving guidance on personal and social education. See *counselling*; *guidance*; *moral education*; *pastoral care*; *social skills*.

phonics   This is a method of helping children to learn to read. It is often contrasted with the *look and say* method, although in practice most teachers tend to use a combination of methods. In a phonic approach teachers concentrate on the way letters sound, encouraging the children to sound out individual sounds within words. In look and say there is more emphasis on the names of letters and the shapes of whole words. See *reading*; *reading schemes*.

Piaget, Jean   Jean Piaget (1896–1980) was a Swiss clinical psychologist who had great influence on world opinion about how children develop and, by implication, how they should be taught. He articulated a stage theory of children's development, broadly the view that children progressed inexorably through a series of stages which were associated with defined behaviours and abilities. He called the stages sensory motor, pre-operational, concrete operational and formal operational. His ideas had great influence in teacher education colleges where they were seen as supporting such ideas as activity-based and *discovery learning*, the concept of readiness to learn and the need to focus on individual children's needs. Critics argued that Piaget's ideas underestimated children's capabilities in the primary years and led to some teachers' expectations of their children being too low.

pilot study A pilot study is a small-scale trial undertaken in advance of a major study. Its purpose may be to test new curriculum materials or research instruments – e.g. questionnaires – and then, if necessary, make modifications or refinements. Overall, the process enables developers to decide on the specific appropriateness of materials or instruments for the intended tasks. See *developmental testing; evaluation; feedback.*

planned behaviour modification programme This is a way of using systematic planning, according to *behaviourist* principles, to bring about positive changes in children's behaviour. It involves close identification of the required behaviour; in an infant school, for example, this might be sharing some paints with other children or working on a task for a certain length of time. The teacher decides on the strategy which will bring about the desired behaviour and the rewards which will follow. See *behavioural objectives; behavioural problems.*

play Children in the early years learn through their play. They talk, act out situations, manipulate materials and interact with other children. They do not separate work and play. Hence early years education is often based upon the planning of play which is intended to extend children's experience. This can lead to misunderstandings since the benefits of play may be indirect and play does not seem like proper schooling. See *kindergarten; playgroups; pre-school education; pre-school playgroup (PPG); structured play; toy libraries.*

play schemes These are schemes arranged for children in school holidays. They may be organised by local education authorities or voluntary bodies. They generally use school premises or parks and are staffed by people taken on for the specific period of play scheme and might include, for example, teachers in training. They provide a varied diet of educational, sporting, cultural and recreational activities.

playgrounds Playgrounds are complex places and not always comfortable ones for all children. There has been some reaction against the bleak, hard feel of old-fashioned playgrounds which amounted to nothing more than an expanse of tarmac. Some schools have begun to devise more interesting playgrounds which resemble parks or recreation and exploration areas. These might have different parts set aside for different activities which are likely to be used by children in smaller groups. There have been some recent experiments in playground architecture and settings which break away from the stereotype of packs of boys playing football in the centre of the play-ground and smaller groups of girls walking warily around the edge.

playgroups   These are organisations which provide opportunities for young children to meet and play with other children before they start school. There is a strong educational focus in the sense that play is seen as the vehicle for early learning. Originally, many playgroups were started up and run voluntarily, often by associations of parents. They are not necessarily led by people holding educational quali-fications. They were in part a response to the low level of *nursery school*, or more formal *pre-school education* provision in England and Wales. The playgroup movement is substantial and may well be more formally recognised within pre-school educational structures in the future. See *childminders*; *pre-school playgroup (PPG)*. For further infor-mation contact:

> The Pre-School Playgroup Association
> 61–63 Kings Cross Road
> London
> WC1X 9LL
>
> Telephone No: 0171 833 0991

Plowden Report   The 1967 Plowden Report made recommenda-tions about the future shape of *primary* education in England. It was chaired by Lady Bridget Plowden and entitled 'Children and Their Primary Schools'. It has been criticised by some new right education commentators for embracing a *progressive* orthodoxy which has led to lower *standards* in schools. The report is a bulky one which is not only concerned with aspects of learning and teaching in school but also relations between schools and parents, the structure of schools for the primary phase and the countering of social disadvantage. It was the final report produced by the Central Advisory Council and is sup-ported by substantial appendices covering a series of empirical stud-ies carried out for the committee. See *first school*; *middle schools*.

Portage scheme   The Portage scheme is for pre-school pupils having learning or development problems. It was originally devel-oped at Portage, Wisconsin and was introduced in Britain in the late 1970s. There are variations in the way schemes operate in detail, but the basic principle is that parents and teachers work together in the home on a carefully planned programme of learning tasks. The teacher will visit the home regularly, usually once a week. A structured programme of small, discrete and manageable tasks is planned and explained to the parents, who are responsible for implementing it. The teacher's main responsibility is to instruct the parents about the tasks. The parents' high level of commitment and support within the scheme is seen as a key ingredient in its success. See *home–school relations*; *learning difficulty*; *special educational needs (SEN)*.

positive discrimination   This term is used to denote the channelling of educational resources to districts or individuals of greatest need. It is a function which requires a district-wide planning body, such as a local education authority, to determine the need and allocate the resources. A term also in widespread use to describe the same idea is *compensatory education*. In other words it is believed that educational provision should compensate for a child's social and economic *disadvantages*. Clearly such an approach to educational resource allocation sits uneasily alongside a more individualistic, competitive, market-led philosophy. See *Head Start*.

Postgraduate Certificate of Education (PGCE)   This is a training route into a teaching career for graduates. It is a course which has usually been taken full-time over one academic year, although part-time schemes have recently been developed. PGCE courses are available for primary and secondary initial teacher training. They are organised and validated by institutions of higher education. See *articled teacher*; *qualified teacher status (QTS)*; *teachers*.

postgraduate studies   After students have received their first *degree*, they sometimes go on to work on further, postgraduate courses. A *graduate* who wishes to teach would normally take the *Postgraduate Certificate in Education* (PGCE) for example. Other graduates might take a course at Masters level, or begin doctoral research towards a PhD. See *dissertation*; *thesis*.

practical assessment   This is the *assessment* of *skills* of a practical nature, undertaken in the practice setting rather than the examination hall. The development of practical assessment is associated with artistic, dramatic, experimental, craft, design, physical and motor skills. It is concerned to assess the *competence* of pupils in various fields of activity. The principle of practical assessment is applied to the area of *vocational* preparation. See *GNVQ* and *NVQ*.

prefect   The prefect system originated in *public schools*. It is a system whereby senior pupils in a school are given special status, and sometimes an insignia of office, so that they can help in maintaining order in the school. The responsibilities vary, but in the *state school* they commonly involve assistance in controlling younger pupils at break and dinner times, supervising corridors and common rooms and generally assisting teachers in the school. The use of prefect systems in state schools has declined and there is more emphasis now on all pupils learning to take responsibility for their own actions. Recourse to an elite group of senior pupils is seen by some as counter-productive.

preparatory schools   These are fee-paying, *private schools* for pupils between the ages of 8 and 13. They are preparatory in the sense that they prepare pupils for entrance to fee-paying *secondary schools* through the *Common Entrance Examination*. Preparatory schools are more often *day schools* rather than *boarding schools*, though both exist. Preparatory schools do not necessarily teach the *National Curriculum*, although some do. The ethos of preparatory schools is predominantly that of the *public school* system as a whole. The curriculum commonly includes French and Latin. See *Incorporated Association of Preparatory Schools (IAPS)*.

pre-preparatory schools   These are *independent*, fee-paying schools for pupils to attend before they enrol in *preparatory schools*.

pre-school education   All education provided for children below the school starting age of five is termed pre-school education. It may be provided in *playgroups* or *nurseries* and organised by *local education authorities* or voluntary bodies. There is increasing awareness of the importance of good early years' education. The report of the independent *National Commission on Education* in 1994, 'Learning to Succeed', made expansion of nursery schools one of its principal objectives. See *day nurseries; Head Start; kindergarten; pre-school playgroup (PPG)*.

pre-school playgroup (PPG)   *Playgroups* operate in the voluntary sector and provide part-time facilities for children who are below the statutory school age. There has been political controversy surrounding the provision of *nursery* and pre-school education. Many official and non-official reports have recognised the importance of increasing the proportion of young children who have access to good pre-school education. There has been dispute about whether this can be fully provided in state funded nursery classes taught by fully qualified teachers and about the contribution which will be made by PPGs.

pressure group   A pressure group is composed of people who hold similar views on a particular issue or cause. The group coordinates the actions of its members in its bid to influence government, people or institutions and strives to force changes in policies and practice. In an age of conscious consumerism, pressure groups in education – e.g. *National Confederation of Parent–Teacher Associations* – monitor events and announcements and advance their causes through conferences, pamphleteering, lobbying and public relations.

primary schools   In England, Wales and Northern Ireland the term primary school refers to education provided for children aged 5 to 11, in Scotland for children aged 5 to 12. The distinctive phase of primary schooling, replacing that of the *elementary* tradition, was made statutory in the 1944 Education Act. Most forms of primary education contain an *infant* stage, sometimes in a separate school, for children aged 5 to 7, and a *junior* stage for children aged 7 to 11. Where provision is in one school it will be termed JMI (junior mixed infants) or primary. In a decreasing number of LEAs there is a different system in operation, with transfer to *secondary schools* at 13. In these LEAs there are *first schools* for children aged 5 to 8 and *middle schools* for children aged 8 to 13. See *age of transfer*; *Butler Act (1944 Education Act)*; *National Association for Primary Education (NAPE)*; *nursery class*; *Plowden Report*.

principal   As a general term, principal usually refers to the head or chief officer of the institution. In *secondary schools* the term is sometimes interchangeable with *headteacher* and in some *universities* it is a title given to the officer who works closely with the *vice-chancellor*. See *Committee of Vice-Chancellors and Principals (CVCP)*.

prison education   All prisons must provide a programme of educational provision. Prison education departments are generally associated with institutions of *further education*. They comprise a core of full-time staff generally supplemented by a team of part-time teachers. Education provision embodies the rehabilitative impulse of penal institutions. It encompasses a wide range of provision, given the wide spread of ability, experience and needs of its clientele. Both vocational and academic education might feature as a part of a prison education programme. There might well be an emphasis, for some inmates, on basic *literacy* and *numeracy*. For others, an academic programme might entail study with the *Open University*.

private schools   See *public schools*.

private tuition   Sometimes parents feel their children would benefit from extra tuition outside school. Such tuition may be informally provided by parents themselves or it may be bought from a private tutor. Many private tutors offer services at key periods of pupils' lives, most noticeably the public examination years of 16 and 18. Many private tutors are ex-teachers or teachers supplementing their incomes. A development of the same impulse is the existence of *'crammers'*, institutions which have become expert in cramming children's minds with material which will help them to pass examinations.

probationary year   The probationary year was a system in place until 1992 whereby newly appointed beginning teachers served a year's probation in a maintained school. LEAs were responsible for reporting successful completion of the probationary year to the Department of Education and Science. The system was abandoned in favour of a process which emphasised individual schools' responsibility for the *induction* of their *newly qualified teachers* (NQTs). See *mentor*.

problem-solving   In this approach to *learning*, pupils have to consider and solve problems at first hand. As learners, they usually try to develop a strategy, apply existing *knowledge* and *skills* and add to them. Some teachers believe that the approach improves pupils' self-confidence and powers of independent thinking. See *convergent thinking*.

Professional Association of Teachers (PAT)   This teachers' association pledges that its members will never strike. See *unions*.

professor   A professor is one of the acknowledged authorities in a subject or broader curriculum area at *university* level. Two types of professorships can be established; the first is a named post or chair, the second can be based on academic reputation or recognition for excellence as a teacher. When the *binary* line in *higher education* (HE) was abolished in 1992 (*Further and Higher Education Act*), the number of professorships increased markedly as polytechnics assumed university status. See *emeritus; honorary degree*.

profile   The profile is a collection of evidence of children's progress and *attainment*. It is intended to be a holistic record of children's learning, emphasising success and achievement. A profile will contain examples of children's work together with teachers' and pupils' comments on each area of the curriculum. It will also contain references to a child's contribution to non-academic areas of the school curriculum, for example sporting, musical and drama activities and to children's *attendance* and *behaviour*. The profile as a means of recording achievement is felt to be informative for pupils, parents and prospective employers. Because it involves pupils in assessing their own strengths and weaknesses, it is seen as a motivating aspect of *assessment*. See *feedback; record of achievement; records*.

profile component (PC)   When the *National Curriculum* was under development there was much talk of profile components as part of the structure of *assessment* and *testing*. These were collections of *attainment targets* in each separate subject grouped together to form the basis of assessment in that subject. The idea was to reduce the large numbers of attainment targets to a more manageable number of profile components which would then be more efficiently assessed. It would then be possible to report children's progress in each profile component and this would aid the construction of comparative *league tables*. See *aggregation*.

programme of study (PoS)   Each subject area in the *National Curriculum* consists of a programme of study. In essence the programme of study is the curriculum followed by the pupil at each *key stage*. In the terminology of the National Curriculum, a programme of study refers to the matters, skills and processes which must be taught to pupils at each key stage in order for them to meet the *objectives* set out in the *attainment targets* for that subject. See *full course; short course; strand; syllabus*.

programmed learning   This is an approach to *instruction* which is based on the preparation of teaching materials, often according to *behaviourist* principles. Programmed learning employs a very gradual sequence of learning steps, regular *feedback* and a logical *progression* through the material to be mastered or understood. The instruction is individual. The principles have been translated to some computer programmes. See *continuity and progression*.

progression   This is a key term in understanding the effectiveness of educational provision. It refers to the way in which teaching is planned to build systematically on pupils' previous learning so that there is development of their capabilities over a period of time. Teachers' planning should ensure that there is progression in each area of the *National Curriculum* within the school year and from year to year. It is important that there is planning for pupils' progression in learning from one *key stage* to another, especially where this involves transfer from one school to another. A well-planned policy for pupils' progression in learning will indicate how their knowledge, concepts, skills and attitudes will be systematically developed through the school curriculum. See *continuity and progression*.

progressive   This term is taken to indicate a certain set of attitudes towards education. It is sometimes seen as a contrast to a traditional educational stance. Progressive education has been criticised by right-wing education commentators who believe it has contributed to a decline in educational standards. The term originated in America at the turn of the century where it was associated with the ideas of John Dewey. Progressive education emphasises the importance of the child's interests and *motivation*. It sees bodies of knowledge as domains to be investigated and dealt with in an integrated rather than a separate way. The term is also taken to denote an attitude towards authority. Whereas traditional education was associated with formal structures and organisation, strong discipline and control, progressive ideas are softer. They see the teacher as a facilitator of learning rather than instructor, emphasise individual and collective endeavour rather than competition and are interested in *child-centredness* rather than teacher-centredness. The problem with the term is that it has become a part of political debate and is often used in a pejorative and unhelpful way. See *Black Papers*; *Hillgate Group*; *Inner London Education Authority (ILEA)*; *New Education Fellowship (NEF)*; *open-plan schools*; *Plowden Report*; *teaching style*.

project   A project is a task which a pupil, or group of pupils, undertakes. In primary schools a project might well be associated with the class *topic* which is being followed. The project will enable children to pursue an aspect of the topic in some depth. It is a form of work intended to allow for some independence in learning and, usually, an element of collaboration. By its nature, a project will be open-ended, requiring children to make decisions about what and what not to pursue. The investigation will normally result in a written, oral or graphical presentation of the outcome. In secondary schools project work has become more common since the development of new approaches to GCSE *coursework*. Despite uneasiness in some quarters, and a feeling that projects and other forms of coursework are less demanding than traditional examinations, teachers have tended to support the use of projects as a part of *assessment*.

prospectus   It is a requirement that all state schools should publish a prospectus for parents. It should set out a picture of the school's policy and character so that parents can make an informed choice about the education of their children. See *information*; *Parents' Charter*; *school policy*.

public schools   This is the odd, English term for an independent, or fee-paying or private school. In Scotland a public school is a *state school*.

There are some 200 public schools in England, many of them *boarding schools*. Their *headteachers* are members of the *Headmasters' Conference*. These schools are responsible for about 7 per cent of the school population. Among reasons for their continuing influence are the excellence of the education provided in the best fee-paying schools, the social advantages parents perceive for their children through attending fee-paying schools, and the high proportion of former public school pupils in responsible and well-paid positions in society. Approximately half the entrants to Oxford and Cambridge universities still come from public schools, despite efforts in recent years to attract more candidates from state schools.

Public schools are not provided with financial resources by the state or LEAs. Many of them were founded through endowments by their founders and now have *charitable status*. There is increasing pressure on some public schools to make money as a business. Hence, there has been a move to appoint general managers rather than teachers as heads of some schools. When the move towards establishing the comprehensive secondary sector was taking place, some former *direct grant grammar schools* became independent.

The public schools tend to have smaller class sizes than state secondary schools. They are not obliged to follow the *National Curriculum*, although some do. Many of the public schools, although a decreasing proportion overall, are still *single-sex schools*. Most offer facilities for children as boarders or on a *day school* basis. In general the proportion of pupils using public schools on a day basis has been increasing. There is still a strongly traditional element in the curriculum of many public schools, both in its academic and non-academic aspects.

Public schools do not necessarily have to employ teachers who have been formally trained with a qualification leading to *QTS* (qualified teacher status), still a requirement to teach in the state sector. Part of the independent sector also encompasses schools for religious minorities such as Quakers and Muslims. There is also a small number of *progressive* institutions in the sector. Independent schools are required to register with the *Department for Education* (DFE). The register is intended to signify that the school meets minimum standards. The *Assisted Places Scheme* was introduced by the Conservative government as a way of enabling children from ordinary families to gain entry to the independent sector. See *boarding schools; Common Entrance Examination; entrance awards; house system; Independent School's Information Service (ISIS); prefect; preparatory schools; pre-preparatory schools*. For further information contact:

Independent Schools Information Service (ISIS)
56 Buckingham Gate
London
SW1E 6AG

Telephone No: 0171 630 8793

punishments *Corporal punishment* is no longer legal in schools, although a variety of other punishments might be used. These include additional work, such as repetitive writing of an appropriate 'line' of text, withdrawal of a privilege of some kind, or withdrawal from a pleasant curriculum activity such as games, and *detention*. See *behaviour; discipline; Society of Teachers Opposed to Physical Punishment (STOPP)*.

pupil A pupil is any person taught by another. In the narrower sense, the definition often refers to children of compulsory school-age. In secondary schools, there is a growing tendency to replace pupil with student. See *student*.

pupil–teacher ratio (PTR) The pupil–teacher ratio is the ratio of pupils to teachers within a school. For example, a PTR of 20:1 indicates one teacher per 20 pupils. Increasingly, the PTR is used as a statistical indicator of resources devoted to education and may be used to assess the performance of LEAs or make comparisons of teaching forces available to primary and secondary phases. The PTR should not be equated with *class size*, since the number of teachers will include all staff including any non-teaching, or part-teaching, *heads* and *deputy heads*. Some schools will decide on a staff deployment policy that entails higher than average class size in order to free-up teaching hours for other tasks, for example working with pupils with *special educational needs*.

~ Q R ~

quadrivium See *trivium*.

qualified teacher status (QTS) Qualified teacher status is attained on completion of a recognised course of *teacher* education and *training* in an institution of *higher education*. The main routes by which teachers attain QTS are the *Postgraduate Certificate of Education* (PGCE) which is normally taken one year full-time and the four year *BEd* or BA/BSc (QTS) route. It has also been possible to attain QTS through enrolment on an *Articled Teacher Scheme*. A formal period of *probation* is no longer a requirement before the award of QTS is made by the *DFE*. See *College of Preceptors; licensed teacher*.

quality This is a much-used term in educational discourse. The government has signalled its own interest in promoting high-quality education, through its Citizens' Charter initiative. Like *standards*, however, the idea of quality is elusive since what appeals to some as high-quality educational provision may not bring universal approbation. The government has put heavy emphasis on market forces and parental choice as a way of improving quality, and on the publication of test results as a way of comparing school performances. There is much less emphasis on attracting high-calibre entrants into the teaching profession, improving the quality of resources available to schools or giving proper attention to quality *in-service education* for teachers. Instead, there is emphasis on external control, with a new inspection framework where schools are inspected every four years against a set of criteria encompassing the official view of quality. A veritable industry of quality assurance in education, disconcertingly, has sprung up, bringing all kinds of arcane distinctions which may or may not bring qualitative benefit. Education is awash with the rhetoric of quality so that the jargon of the production line – quality control, quality audit, total quality management and quality assurance – has become common. See *British Standard BS 5750; Parents' Charter*.

quango A quango is a committee set up by the government and given responsibility for managing an aspect of public policy. It is a faintly pejorative term which means quasi-autonomous non-governmental organisation. The use of quangos in parts of the educational system has been criticised on the grounds that members are appointed by the government and may reflect a small spectrum of views conforming to the government's own predispositions and ideological assumptions. There is also a concern that quangos can exercise power without visible accountability. Examples of educational quangos are the *School Curriculum and Assessment Authority* and the *Teacher Training Agency*.

race The question of race relations in schools is a critical one for the development of our society. It is unlawful to discriminate against individuals on account of their race. The 1976 Race Relations Act prohibits schools from discriminating on school admissions or in any other way within the school. Yet there is little doubt that schools are painful arenas where direct and indirect racism can flourish. It is necessary for a whole *school policy* on race to be in place, and not just in those parts of the country where there is a high proportion of children with multi-ethnic backgrounds. See *deficit model; Equal Opportunities Commission; ethnic minorities; hidden curriculum; multicultural education; National Anti-Racist Movement in Education (NAME)*. For further information contact:

> The Commission for Racial Equality
> Elliot House
> 10–12 Allington Street
> London
> SW1E 5EH
>
> Telephone No: 0171 828 7022

Raising of the School Leaving Age (ROSLA) This was a campaign to raise the school leaving age to 16, and it was achieved in 1972–3. See *school leaving age*.

Rampton Report This was a committee of inquiry established in 1979 to consider the education of *ethnic minorities*. The chairman was Sir Anthony Rampton and the report was issued in 1981. The report focused on the *underachievement* of some ethnic minorities, in particular West Indian children, and on the comparatively better performance of Asian children in England and Wales. Discussions of some of the explanations for these differences were controversial since they drew attention to aspects of racism which appeared to be endemic in some schools. See *deficit model*; *disadvantaged*; *race*.

rank   A rank order lists children according to their achievement in certain areas of the curriculum. A *summative* rank order will sum up the achievements of children in all areas of the curriculum in order to identify who is top or bottom of the class. See *cut-off point*; *league tables*.

readability   The idea of assessing the readability of a passage or text is to make sure that children are not given *reading* material which is too difficult for them. There are some formal procedures, for example the readability formula devised by Rudolf Flesch in 1948, designed to assess the readability of text. These are chiefly dependent on the difficulty of individual words and sentence complexity. See *Cloze procedure*; *reading age*.

reader   A reader is a collection of extracts from various sources arranged into a single collection of readings. It is a device commonly used to support courses in *higher education*, particularly those organised by the *Open University* whose students do not have uniformly good access to well-stocked libraries.

readiness   The idea of readiness is that, because of their stage of development, level of *maturation* and educational experiences, children will be ready to move to another learning experience. It is a term used in relation to the teaching of *reading* (reading readiness), although it has been criticised as leading some teachers to be insufficiently interventionist in moving children on to new learning.

reading   An intense debate about the best way of teaching reading in primary schools has been under way for some time. There is concern because of evidence (for example from the *National Foundation for Educational Research*) of decline in the reading performance of primary school children. Critics of current approaches to the teaching of reading say there has been too little emphasis on a *phonic* approach, too little use of *reading schemes* and too much note taken of those who advocate an approach which emphasises the children's use of real books even at the early stages of learning to read. Traditional approaches have combined *look and say* with phonics, all introduced within the context of carefully graded reading schemes. See *basic skills*; *Bullock Report*; *dyslexia*; *flashcards*; *literacy*; *paired reading*; *spelling*; *three Rs*.

reading age   A child's reading age is calculated using various tests of reading ability. These require a child to demonstrate reading competence by reading a piece of connected prose, or by word recognition, or by selecting words to complete sentences. Testers are given strict instructions about testing procedures so that the results are reliable. Reading tests have been developed with large samples of children. They enable a child's progress in reading to be compared with other children of the same age. The result of a reading test is usually calculated as a child's reading age, which may then be compared with the child's *chronological age*. Thus a child of 9 with a reading age of 11 is developing very good skills in reading whereas a reading age of 7 would indicate grounds for concern about that child's progress in reading. See *Cloze procedure; dyslexia; screening*.

reading schemes   These are sets of books intended to help children through the early stage of learning to read. The chief characteristics of reading schemes are a carefully controlled vocabulary, enabling children to learn new words gradually, and grading the books in gently ascending levels of difficulty. Reading schemes might employ either the *look and say* method of teaching reading or a *phonic* approach, or elements of both. Critics of reading schemes argue that they are necessarily artificial and repetitive, failing to engage children's real interests in books. See *paired reading; readability; reading*.

reception class   This is the *class* which children join at the beginning of their time in the *infant school* when they are aged five or under. In some schools children start to attend reception classes on a part-time basis. See *rising fives*.

record of achievement   The record of achievement is the cumulative record of a pupil's academic, personal and social progress over a stage of education. At the end of a pupil's school career it is the document which contains evidence of the pupil's achievement and personal qualities. The *National Record of Achievement* (NRA) is intended for all pupils aged 16 and is available for employers and interviewers at the next stage of education. Records of achievement began to be developed in the 1970s and became compulsory in 1993. See *profile*.

records   Records must be kept on every pupil in a maintained school. They must include material on academic achievements, other skills and abilities and progress in school. They must be updated at least once a year. Access to the records, subject to any exempt material, must be given to the pupil's *parents*, the pupil if over 16 and to any school or further education establishment considering the pupil for admission, or to which the pupil transfers. *Assessment* results may be disclosed to another school only after the pupil has been admitted to that school. Records must include the results of National Curriculum assessment at 7, 11, 14 and 16. See *information*; *National Record of Achievement*; *profile*; *reports*.

redbrick university The term originated to denote *universities* built in the cities – civic universities such as Leeds, Manchester and Birmingham – at the turn of the century. The point of the term was to contrast these new, civic universities with Oxford and Cambridge.

registered inspector A registered inspector is deemed competent to engage in the inspection of schools under the terms of the 1992 Education (Schools) Act. Under Section 9 of this Act the Chief Inspector of Schools (HMCI) keeps a register of the *inspectors* who are recognised by *OFSTED*. See *Her Majesty's Inspectorate (HMI)*; *inspection team member*; *Office of Her Majesty's Chief Inspector of Schools*.

registrar A registrar is responsible for such aspects of administration in an academic organisation as student applications, records and examinations. See *ancillary staff*; *support staff*.

regression The term is used in at least two ways. First, it denotes behaviour which has regressed to a previous stage of development. Explanations of regressive behaviour may be of interest to teachers and psychologists. Second, regression to the mean is a statistical concept which describes the tendency for examination and other marks to cluster around the average no matter what the range of marks may have been. See *standard deviation*; *Z-scores*.

reliability The term is commonly applied to educational tests or measurements. The question of reliability refers to a judgement of whether a test would yield the same results if it were administered on different occasions with broadly similar samples of children. See *validity*.

remedial teaching Remedial teaching aims to give children special help when they are experiencing *learning difficulties*. Its use is limited today when terms like *support teacher*, integration and *special needs* are more popular. Remedial teachers are traditionally associated with the policy of extracting children who were slow learners to receive special attention individually, in small groups or sometimes in selective classes. The practice is now little used. See *learning support; Warnock Report; withdrawal.*

reports   Schools must provide a written report for *parents* at least once a year. The report must provide notes on a pupil's progress in all subjects studied as a part of the school's curriculum. It will also contain details of the pupil's general progress and performance in all *National Curriculum assessments* and public *examinations;* an *attendance* record; school and national comparative information about National Curriculum assessments and public examinations and details of the arrangements whereby the report may be discussed with teachers. In sum, the purpose of reports is to communicate to parents significant and relevant *information* on the individual pupil's experience and achievements. There are four points at which pupil performance is reported in relation to National Curriculum levels or *end of key stage statements.* These are at or near the end of each key stage when most pupils will be 7, 11, 14 or 16. See *feedback; Parents' Charter; profile.*

resources for learning   These are the range of book and non-book resources which schools use to further pupil *learning.* Non-book resources include video, *IT,* audio material, posters, artifacts, worksheets and materials for various kinds of art, *craft and design* activities. Resources for learning encompass the school and local environment, special locations for learning (such as a swimming pool or athletics track) and contact with adult non-teachers. Under *LMS* schools are responsible for providing their own resources for learning. It is widespread for *PTAs* to be involved in fundraising to provide resources which would otherwise be beyond the school's ability to provide. See *pupil–teacher ratio; teachers' centres.*

rising fives   These are children who have not quite reached the school starting age of five but who are sometimes admitted to *reception classes.* Policy on rising fives varies from one local educational authority to another. Parents are sometimes very keen for their four-year-olds to start school, but it is generally acknowledged that care is needed in selecting appropriate educational activities for very young children in the *infant* classroom. See *school milk.*

Robbins Report   This was an important part of the post-war educational settlement, a vision of the future of *higher education* in the United Kingdom. Robbins (1963) argued for a massive expansion of higher education provision, an increase in the number of students entering *university* and a substantial building programme of new universities. The assumption on which the report was based was that a university place would be open to each student qualified to receive it. It was argued that the pool of national talent had been severely underestimated in the past. Specific proposals included the redesignation of *teacher training* colleges as *colleges of education*, with closer links with the universities, and increasing the status of the colleges of advanced technology.

rote learning   This approach emphasises learning facts or ideas mechanically by repetition, or by heart. Its use was associated with the old *elementary* tradition and conjures up images of children singing out their times *tables* or remembering all the capital cities of the world. Rote learning is criticised because it pays no attention to the idea that learning should be meaningful or that we need to understand what we learn. Upholders of the rote learning tradition argue that it symbolises a kind of discipline in learning and that some useful facts, such as tables, can only be learned by rote. See *active learning*; *passive learning*.

Royal Society of Arts (RSA)   The RSA offers examinations in a number of *vocational* subject areas, thus its qualifications are most widely used in *further education*. Together with the *City and Guilds of London Institute* (CGLI), the RSA has been at the forefront of the development of vocational qualifications. See *Certificate of Pre-Vocational Education*; *GNVQ*; *NVQ*.

Rutter, Michael   The Rutter Report, 'Fifteen Thousand Hours', was written by Michael Rutter and his colleagues and published in 1979. Its title refers to the total length of time a pupil spends in school and is a study of the processes and effects of *secondary schooling*. It is significant because its findings contradicted previous, influential research which was pessimistic about the influence of schools. Rutter began to identify those aspects of a school's ethos, management and policies which were associated with high pupil achievement and good behaviour. The book was influential and an early example of *school effectiveness* and school improvement research in England and Wales.

S level   S level is used to indicate the high level of the examination paper that can be taken by *GCE A level* students of high *ability*. The examinations, and those who pass them, are highly regarded by admissions tutors in *higher education* institutions.

sandwich course   This is a term used to signify periods of study spent in an educational institution interspersed with periods of practice spent in a workplace. A sandwich course is seen as a useful model for vocational training. See *vocational education*.

scholarship   A scholarship is an award which carries entry to an educational institution combined with a sum of money. A scholarship is normally won through success in an open competitive examination. See *entrance awards*.

School-Centred Initial Teacher Training (SCITT)   This new form of training, established in 1993, enables individual schools and school consortia to provide courses of initial *teacher training*. The policy is controversial since it does not require *higher education* institutions to be involved. Although there were initially very few students enrolled on SCITT courses an objective of the government's *Teacher Training Agency* is to increase school-centred training.

School Certificate   This qualification for 16-year-olds was introduced in 1917 and remained until 1951 when *GCE O level* certification replaced it. The School Certificate examination was the culmination of a four-year course for some *secondary* pupils and, in order to gain the award, candidates had to pass in five subjects.

school closure   Under the 1980 Education Act the *local education authorities* intending to close a school have to give parents two months' notice in which to object. Closure notices are frequently applied to village schools. If there are no objections the LEA can simply close the school. If there are objections the case is referred to the *Secretary of State*. It is noticeable that schools under threat of closure are applying for *grant maintained status*, since GM schools cannot be closed by LEAs. See *Section 12 Notice*.

school council This is a forum where pupil and teacher representatives put their points of view on aspects of school life. Pupil representatives are normally elected by fellow pupils, although in some cases they may be nominated by teachers. They are not a legal requirement and will not be a feature of all schools.

School Curriculum and Assessment Authority (SCAA) The SCAA was established in October 1993 as the government's *curriculum* and *assessment* advisory board. It succeeded the *National Curriculum Council* (NCC) and the *Schools Examination and Assessment Council* (SEAC), in effect merging their functions. See *Curriculum and Assessment Authority for Wales (ACAC); Dearing, Sir Ron*. For further information contact:

SCAA
Newcombe House
45 Notting Hill Gate
London
W11 3JB

Telephone No: 0171 229 1234

school day The length of the school day is determined by school governors. There are no legal requirements although guidance from the DFE suggests 21 hours per week for children aged 5 to 7, 23.5 for those aged 8 to 11 and 24 for those aged 12 to 16. Recent evidence from HMI suggested wide variation in the length of school days among schools and there has been talk of introducing legislation to meet this concern. In England and Wales the common position is for a school day starting around nine o'clock and finishing around a quarter to four, with a break for lunch and two shorter breaks in the morning and afternoon. There have been some experiments with the idea of a continental school day, starting earlier in the morning, having less time for breaks and dinner and ending much earlier in the day. Such an arrangement has consequences for the *child care* arrangements of many *parents*. See *after-school activities; extended day; extra-curricular activities; staff meeting; timetable*.

school development plan (SDP)   This is a plan which identifies improvements needed in curriculum, organisation, staffing and resources needed by a school. It also sets out the actions which are needed to make those improvements. It is written by the headteacher, in consultation with teachers and, increasingly, governors. See *school policy; zero budgeting approach.*

school effectiveness   Since the early 1980s there has been much interest in identifying the factors which help to explain the effectiveness of schools. An influential report on secondary schools, 'Fifteen Thousand Hours', summed up work by Michael *Rutter* and colleagues on secondary schools' performance. A similarly influential report on primary schools, 'School Matters', was produced by Peter Mortimore and colleagues. The interesting point is that both these pieces of work, and others which followed, ended the pessimistic view that schools did not really make a great deal of difference to the educational outcome of children with similar abilities and home backgrounds. By looking carefully at such features as *management* and leadership, school policies, attitudes to *homework*, the ethos of the school, *attendance* and *truancy* levels, and a host of others, this school effectiveness research began to consider the characteristics of the most effective schools. See *performance indicators; value added.*

school health service   School health services are organised within the National Health Service. The people who undertake work in schools as part of a school health team are the school nurse, school dentist and school doctor. Members of the team are likely to make visits to school from time to time to monitor aspects of children's health. See *health education.*

school leaving age   The school leaving age is 16. This was established in the academic year 1972–3 when the *Raising of the School Leaving Age* (ROSLA) campaign achieved its objective. At present there is no substantive campaign to extend compulsory schooling beyond the age of 16, although some aspects of *Youth Training* (YT) are beginning to develop a feeling of compulsion. See *Butler Act (1944 Education Act).*

School Library Association (SLA)   The Association encourages good practice in the development of school libraries. See *Library Association.* For further information contact:

School Library Association
Liden Library
Barrington Close
Liden
Swindon
Wiltshire
SN3 6HF

Telephone No: 01793 617838

School Library Service (SLS)   The SLS is a system of support for teachers organised by the local authority. It allows stocks of books to be borrowed for particular purposes, often in connection with particular projects or topics, on a rotating basis. It is a particularly useful service for small schools.

school management team   As part of schools' increasing concern with good *management* practice it has become common for secondary schools to establish a formal school management team to oversee policy and its implementation. The *head*, *deputy head*(s) and heads of *faculty* would normally belong to the management team and sometimes, in addition, the school's senior administration officer. In primary schools such a formal arrangement of a designated senior management group is rare.

school meals   The provision of school meals was made a legal requirement of local education authorities under the 1944 Act, a state of affairs which continued until 1980. Local education authorities are still statutorily bound to provide meals for the children of parents on income support, but are under no obligation to provide meals for all children. There has been concern about the effects on children's nutrition of the collapse of the old-style school meals service in favour of cafeteria systems offering children the opportunity to select fast foods or packed lunches. See *competitive tendering*.

school milk   School milk for all *primary* children was a feature of the national sense of responsibility for children's healthy growth following the Second World War. By stages, since 1979, the provision of free milk has been removed, at first from all children except those from families receiving income support and then in 1988 from all children except the under-fives. It is currently an entitlement of children in *state schools* who have not yet reached the age of five. See *nursery class*; *rising fives*.

school nurse   See *school health service*.

school phobia   The condition of school phobia occurs when an individual is unable to bear the prospect of going to school. It is normally applied to pupils rather than teachers.

school policy   This is an agreed statement about the general aims or *mission* of the school, often presented to parents as a part of the school *prospectus*. The school will also normally have a *development plan*, drawn up by the governing body, which outlines the ways in which the school expects to further its aims. Each area of the curriculum will have its own statement of policy drawn up by departmental staff in a secondary school and by the curriculum coordinator and other teachers in a primary school. See *information; school development plan*.

school psychological service   The school psychological service consists of a team of *educational psychologists* employed by the LEA. Their function is to assist schools in the diagnosis and assessment of children with *special educational needs*, including the procedure of *statementing*. Most educational psychologists have been teachers and have undertaken undergraduate work in psychology and postgraduate work in psychology applied to education. See *diagnostic assessment*.

school secretary   A linch pin of the effective school, the school secretary frequently operates as personal assistant to the head, clerk, keeper of accounts, first aider, and confidant to parents and staff. In larger schools there will be more prospect of division of roles among a substantial office but in small primary schools the duties will tend to fall on one person's desk. The increased responsibility of schools for their own financial management has led to greatly increased duties, akin to those of *bursar*, for some school secretaries. While larger schools have in many cases been able to increase the level of administrative support, primary schools have generally had to rely on voluntary help or ask even more of hard-pressed and poorly paid secretarial *support staff*. See *ancillary staff*.

school visit   School visits and trips are a feature of the curriculum of most schools. There is normally a charge. Some visits may be associated with part of a formal curriculum, for example field work in geography or science. Other visits may be part of the school's commitment to enrich children's cultural lives, for example a theatre or concert visit. It is also common for schools to organise sporting fixtures, which involve travel, skiing trips to Europe and residential trips of various kinds. Schools are necessarily careful about the organisation of such visits, particularly in the area of pupil safety. Parents' written permission must be obtained before pupils go on a school visit. See *exchange schemes; extra-curricular activities; field study; museums.*

Schools Examination and Assessment Council (SEAC)   SEAC was established under the 1988 *Education Reform Act* to advise the *Secretary of State* and keep under review all aspects of *examinations* and *assessment.* It was a separate body from the *National Curriculum Council.* SEAC and the NCC were abolished in 1993 and replaced by the *School Curriculum and Assessment Authority* (SCAA), a national body designed to bring the responsibility to advise on the *National Curriculum* and assessment within one organisation. See *levels of attainment.*

Schools Funding Agency   See *Funding Agency for Schools.*

Scotland: Five to Fourteen Development Programme   The *National Curriculum* only applies to England and Wales. The Scottish Five to Fourteen Development Programme is advisory rather than statutory. It offers guidelines about good practice and is much less prescriptive than the English version. The Development Programme is based on five areas in the primary school: language, mathematics, expressive arts, environmental education and religious and moral education. The secondary school has eight areas: language and communication, mathematics, science, social and environmental studies, technology, creative and aesthetic activities, PE and religious and moral education. See *Munn Report.*

Scottish Certificate of Education (SCE)   The SCE is the equivalent secondary leaving qualification to *GCSE* and *A level.* At 16, Scottish pupils take the standard grade SCE and at 18 the higher grade.

Scottish Office Education Department (SOED)   This is the office with responsibility for education in Scotland. The functions are the same as those for the *DFE* in England and Wales. For further information contact:

Scottish Office Education Department (SOED)
New St Andrew's House
St James' Centre
Edinburgh
EH1 3SY

Telephone No: 0131 556 8400

screening   Screening is undertaken to identify pupils – or groups of pupils – for particular purposes. It can be a time-consuming exercise and is not undertaken lightly. It is used most commonly to establish profiles of *learning difficulties* in reading, writing and mathematics. Teachers can make use of a variety of tests for diagnosing difficulties encountered by pupils who have disabilities. See *diagnostic assessment; reading age; special educational needs (SEN)*.

Secondary Heads Association (SHA)   The Association is a professional body for *headteachers* and *deputy headteachers*. It was formed from two previous bodies, the Headmasters' Association and the Association of Headmistresses, in 1976, and offers membership to heads and deputies in *independent* and *maintained schools*. The Association provides a forum for discussion on matters affecting all schools and makes known its views on new developments. See *unions*.

secondary modern school   Secondary modern schools were one part of the *tripartite* system established under the 1944 Education Act; the others were *grammar* and *technical schools*. The secondary modern schools suffered low esteem in the eyes of many parents, children and teachers by comparison with the selective grammar schools. From the 1970s secondary modern schools were generally reorganised into *comprehensive schools*. See *bilateral school; bipartite system; Butler Act (1944 Education Act); multilateral education*.

secondary school   This is a school catering for pupils after the age of 11 in the majority of cases, though in some areas with *middle schools* the *age of transfer* to the secondary phase may occur at 12 or 13. There are various kinds of secondary schools. The majority are *comprehensive*, in other words they cater for pupils of all abilities and are not *selective*. However selective *grammar schools* still exist in some parts of the country. Secondary schools may be *independent, grant maintained* or under the aegis of local education authorities. They may be denominational or non-denominational. Some are divided into lower and upper schools. Some cater exclusively for the age range 11 to 16, while others cater for the full 11 to 18 range and have sixth forms. See *bilateral school*; *City Technology Colleges (CTCs)*; *eleven-plus examination*; *tripartite system*.

secondment   A teacher may be given a period of leave to follow a professional or academic course – i.e. secondment. Alternatively, a teacher may be asked to fill temporarily a post in another school – although under current local management of schools (LMS) and grant maintained arrangements, local education authorities are less inclined to arrange secondments of this kind.

Secretary of State   This is a shorter term generally in use to describe the Secretary of State for Education. With regard to Wales, the Secretary of State acts in conjunction with the Secretary of State for Wales. In Scotland responsibility for education lies with the Secretary of State for Scotland. The Secretary of State for Education is responsible for the work of the *Department for Education* and for the formulation and implementation of its policies. The Secretary of State is responsible for education in schools, further education and the university sector. To undertake these tasks the Secretary of State is assisted by a minister of state and two parliamentary junior ministers (under-secretaries of state). See *circulars*; *Department of Education Northern Ireland (DENI)*; *Scottish Office Education Department (SOED)*; *Welsh Office Education Department (WOED)*. For further information contact:

> Secretary of State for Education
> Sanctuary Buildings
> Great Smith Street
> London
> SW1P 3BT
>
> Telephone No: 0171 925 5000

Section 11 staff   These are teachers and non-teaching assistants whose specific function is to provide language and *learning support* for pupils of New Commonwealth heritage. These posts are additional to the school's staffing establishment. The funding is in response to *LEA* and school bids and up to 75 per cent is provided by the Home Office under the 1966 Local Government Act. See *bilingual assistants*; *bilingual pupils*; *ethnic minorities*; *partnership teaching*.

Section 12 Notice A Section 12 Notice is part of the procedure brought into play when a local education authority is seeking to close a school. Section 12 of the 1980 Education Act requires LEAs to issue a notice giving public notice of the closure and inviting objections. See *school closure*.

selection Selection normally refers to a process through which children are selected, normally on the basis of a written *test*, for a particular *secondary school*. The most widespread form of selection of this kind was the *eleven-plus examination*, the basis upon which entrants were selected for *grammar schools* until the 1970s. The educational reforms of the 1980s have not reintroduced selection, although they have introduced the means by which selection could become a school's policy. The legislation would allow a *grant maintained school* to adopt a selective entry procedure.

selective schools These are schools which operate and admissions policy which is designed to select certain kinds of pupils, normally those who have reached a defined level of *attainment*. See *bipartite system*; *grammar schools*; *non-selective schools*.

self-esteem The value or worth of self, as judged by an individual, is central to understanding self-esteem. The processes are complex; esteem may stem from feelings associated with success or failure and believing that others may hold positive or negative views (of that individual). Self-esteem is closely related to self-concept, i.e. the image that the individual has of himself or herself. Some educationalists believe that self-esteem is a potent factor in learning but there is no definitive evidence to suggest that low self-esteem is a conclusive cause of *underachievement* or poor attainment.

self-fulfilling prophecy Sometimes known as the Pygmalion effect after the work of Rosenthal and Jacobson, the idea is that children come to conform to the view of them held by teachers, no matter how accurate or inaccurate that view may be. The implication is that a pupil who is systematically criticised, or made to feel dull, will become so, whereas children who are treated as intelligent achievers begin to conform to that more optimistic expectation. See *halo effect*; *labelling*; *streaming*.

self-governing schools See *grant maintained schools*.

semester The semester is an alternative way of organising the academic year. It is based on the idea of breaking the year into two, rather than the three-term system commonly in use in England and Wales. The semester system is popular in the USA. British *universities* are beginning to adopt semesters too, normally two 15-week semesters.

seminar A seminar is conducted by a *tutor* or teacher to facilitate exposition or discussion in groups; subjects for exposition or discussion may arise from preparatory reading, students' own presentations or lead lectures.

serial practice See *block practice*.

Service Children's Education Authority (SCEA) The provision, administration and staffing of schools for children of armed forces' personnel in overseas bases is the responsibility of the Service Children's Education Authority (SCEA) and the Authority, in turn, is the responsibility of the Ministry of Defence. Teachers recruited to the Authority's schools retain civilian status and, in most respects, schools are organised and run along the same lines as those in England and Wales. SCEA also advises on the possibility of, and financial assistance for, boarding school placements in the United Kingdom for children of services' personnel. For further information contact:

> SCEA
> Director General Adjutant General's Corp
> Worthy Down
> Winchester
> Hampshire
> SO21 2RG
>
> Telephone No: 01962 887965

setting This is a form of grouping. The children are grouped by *ability* for their lessons in a particular subject. In other subjects they may be in different sets or work in *mixed-ability groups*. See *banding*; *class*; *streaming*.

sex education School governing bodies are responsible for determining their schools' policies about sex education. All schools must teach those aspects of sex education contained in *National Curriculum* science, but plans beyond that must be agreed by governing bodies.

They must maintain a written record of those plans and of the content and organisation of any sex education they decide to provide. Any sex education provided by a school must be given in such a way that it encourages pupils to have an understanding of moral considerations and the value of family life. The Local Government Act of 1988 (*Clause 28*) prevents schools from promoting homosexuality. See *health education; moral education; personal and social education; spiritual, moral, social and cultural development*.

sexism   This refers to discrimination against a person because of his or her – most commonly her – gender. It embraces a wide spectrum of institutional and individual patterns of behaviour from overt sexist abuse and contempt, to treating boys and girls differently and having different expectations of them because of their gender. The school curriculum is a potent arena for sexist attitudes, for example, mathematics and science may be regarded as hard, masculine subjects while English and literature may be seen as softer, more feminine areas of study. Some teachers may tolerate or encourage rough, noisy play from boys and inculcate a kind of passive conformity in girls. There is good evidence that boys are more dominant and assertive in mixed-sex classes in school. It may also be the case that institutional hierarchies, with more male teachers in positions of authority in school, often in institutions which have a majority of female teachers, reinforce role models and implicitly reinforce stereotypical expectations of career progression in girls. Concerns about sexist attitudes in some secondary schools have led some parents to consider the possible advantages of *single-sex schools*. It is important to acknowledge that boys, too, can be the victims of sexist attitudes, being denigrated on account of behaviour or interests which do not conform to stereotypical expectations. See *co-education; Equal Opportunities Commission; hidden curriculum*.

short course   This is a course in a *National Curriculum foundation subject* at *Key Stage 4* which will not by itself lead to a *GCSE* or equivalent qualification. Two short courses in different subjects may be combined to form a GCSE or equivalent course. A short course requires about half the teaching time of a full course and has a reduced *programme of study* based on the full course. See *combined course*.

shortage subject   This refers to subjects where there is a shortage of qualified teachers. Recent shortage subjects in secondary education have included mathematics, science and modern languages. A variety of policy initiatives has been introduced to try to deal with the problem, including enhanced *bursaries* for student teachers taking shortage subjects, accelerated undergraduate courses for mature students and marketing campaigns. There is controversy about any proposal to give higher pay to teachers of shortage subjects, simply because they have expertise in a marketable subject area. However, schools do have flexibility in deciding where posts carrying an additional salary *allowance* are located in the school. See *bursary scheme*.

single-sex schools   In the 1960s it was common for primary schools to be of mixed sex and for secondary schools to be single sex. The move to *comprehensive* secondary education involved a shift to mixed sex schools in the overwhelming majority of schools. But a small minority of single-sex schools survived in the *state* sector and remained the normal pattern in the *independent* sector. There has been a revival of interest in the effect of single-sex schools, particularly in respect of girls' academic attainment in general and their performance in specific subjects such as maths and science. See *co-education; sexism*.

sink schools   This term originated in America and describes run-down, underfunded, last-choice schools in a competitive education system. One of the criticisms of the 1988 Education Act is that its drive to bring the discipline of the market into British education, where money follows the child and parental choice is increased, will lead to the sink school phenomenon in this country too.

sixth form college   A sixth form college caters for students who are aged 16 to 18 undertaking sixth form study, predominantly *A levels*. The sixth form college should be distinguished from the *tertiary college* which provides a broader range of academic and *vocational* courses for the whole post-16 population. See *Association for Colleges (AFC)*.

skill   It is widely believed that skill and *ability* are interchangeable terms; as a cognitive, social or physical ability, therefore, skill may be acquired and developed through practice but acquisition and development may be inseparable from *motivation*, understanding, *attitudes* and *knowledge*. See *basic skills; social skills*.

Skinner, B.F.   The work of B.F. Skinner, an American psychologist, gave much impetus to the behaviourist theory of learning as interpreted in schools. See *behaviourism*.

small schools   There has been increasing interest in the work, opportunities and problems of small schools. Sometimes this is because of the problems which occur when *LEAs* seek to close small rural schools, where there may be surplus places. Sometimes it may be that curriculum organisation and delivery is of interest in a human scale of organisation. See *school closure; village schools*. A number of groups have an established interest in small schools. For further information contact:

> National Association for the Support of Small Schools (NASSS)
> The Cottage
> Little Barningham
> Norwich
> NR11 7LN
>
> Telephone No: 01263 775533
>
> Action With Communities in Rural Schools
> Somerford Court
> Somerford Road
> Cirencester
> GL7 1TW
>
> Telephone No: 01285 653477
>
> Human Scale Education Movements
> 96 Carlingcott
> Near Bath
> BA2 8AW
>
> Telephone No: 01761 433733
>
> Small Schools Network
> School of Education
> University of Exeter
> Exeter
> EX1 2LU
>
> Telephone No: 01395 513401

social services   See *child abuse; day nurseries; education welfare officer* (EWO).

social skills   Social and interpersonal *skills* are interrelated. In social situations in schools, colleges and workplaces, successful participants communicate sensitively and effectively. Thus, pupils and students need to practise these skills. See *collaborative/cooperative groupwork; personal and social education* (PSE).

Society of Education Officers (SEO)   This is an organisation for educational administrators. For further information contact:

> Society of Education Officers
> 20 Bedford Way
> London
> WC1H 0AL
>
> Telephone No: 0171 612 6388

Society of Teachers Opposed to Physical Punishment (STOPP)   This is an organisation of teachers and other sympathisers who oppose the use of physical *punishment* in schools. The group was formed to campaign for the elimination of *corporal punishment*, an objective achieved when corporal punishment was stopped in state schools in 1986.

spatial ability   This ability enables learners to perceive spatial relationships between objects. Thus, learners who have a high level of this ability may find it easier to complete jigsaws or similar puzzles, design plans or read maps. Spatial ability is sometimes tested in *aptitude* and *vocational* tests.

special educational needs (SEN)   This refers to pupils who, for a variety of intellectual, physical, sensory, social, emotional or psychological reasons, experience *learning difficulties* which are significantly greater than those experienced by the majority of pupils of the same age. The *Warnock Report* (1978) suggested that up to 20 per cent of children might have these kinds of learning difficulties. Warnock also envisaged support for very able pupils so that their particular needs could be better met. The responsibility for providing help to support children with special needs lies with LEAs. The system which has developed involves the *statement* of special educational needs. This is a summary of the individual's learning difficulties and a proposed plan of action to deal with them. The theory is to provide a more rounded view of the child's needs, including the involvement of parents in the process. In practice, the system has been slow and poorly resourced. Some parents have been reluctant to have their children 'statemented'. The responsibility of governors to provide for pupils with special needs is difficult to put into operation without additional resources. The policy for most pupils with special educational needs is to integrate them in mainstream schools. However, for some children there may still be a need to attend special schools or *special units* attached to ordinary schools where more specialist teaching is available.

All pupils in maintained schools should follow the *National Curriculum* to the maximum extent possible, but the application of its provisions may be *disapplied* or *modified* in relation to pupils with statements of special educational needs. The head of a maintained school may direct that the provisions of the National Curriculum shall not apply, or only with modifications, to a pupil without a statement for a maximum period of six months. The head may also revoke a direction or extend its operative period. Prescribed information must be given by the head to the governors, LEA and pupil's parents. In 1994 a new *code of practice* was introduced in respect of certain procedures for pupils with special needs. See *compensatory education; diagnostic assessment; Down's syndrome; dyslexia; educational psychologists; emotional and behavioural difficulties (EBD); in-class support; learning support; learning support service (LSS); Portage scheme; remedial teaching; school psychological service; screening; special support assistants; support teachers; welfare assistants; withdrawal.*

special schools   These are schools provided for groups of children with particular kinds of *special educational needs*. There are particular regulations pertaining to the approval of special schools, the premises, *assessments* and *statementing*, staffing and the misconduct of teachers and others working with children and young people. Special schools have a lower staff–student ratio (SSR) than maintained schools and they normally provide for the full age range from 5 to 16. Some special schools are residential whilst others operate on a day basis.

special support assistants   These are non-teaching staff who assist teachers to help teach pupils with *statements* of *SEN*. The help is normally provided within the child's classroom rather than in a special facility. See *in-class support; learning support; support staff.*

special units   These are units for the teaching of pupils with *special educational needs*. They are usually provided within specialist accommodation attached to, or a part of, a maintained school. The philosophy of such units is that children attend them for a period of time before going back to their usual class. See *withdrawal.*

specialist teacher assistant (STA)   The STA is an unqualified teaching assistant but undertakes a course to 'specialise' in assisting the teacher in the classroom at *Key Stage* 1. Courses for STAs are currently being piloted in a number of locations throughout the country.

specific grants   These provide funding which is given for particular requirements. For example, the *DFE* provides money for the education of *travellers' children*.

speech therapist   This is an expert in the skill of helping children to improve their speech. Where children have speech defects it is the responsibility of the local education authority to provide speech therapy. See *statement*. For further information contact:

> Association of Speech-Impaired Children
> 347 Central Markets
> Smithfield
> London
> EC1A 9NH
>
> Telephone No: 0171 236 3632

spelling   Schools use a variety of ways of helping children to learn spelling. In the early years, classroom objects may be labelled and there will commonly be an emphasis on working with children on groups of words with similar endings (e.g. night, fight, light). As children learn to *read*, they will begin to remember simple words and recognise when they make mistakes writing them down. Spelling tests of increasing complexity are a feature of most primary classrooms. In the junior years children will begin to use dictionaries more systematically and will have experience of keeping their own spelling lists. Teacher's expectations of accuracy in grammar and spelling will increase and there may well be an emphasis on drafting and redrafting work. School policy on spelling is one of those features of school life which can be taken as symbolic of a general educational philosophy. Right-wing commentators on education have asserted that emphasis on spelling has declined in primary schools but it is difficult to substantiate this claim. See *basic skills*; *Standard English*.

spiral curriculum   This model of the *curriculum* was suggested by Jerome Bruner in order to explain how some *learning* takes place. The curriculum, he claimed, could be arranged so that the learner could come into contact with the same *knowledge* at different times; successive contacts would enhance the knowledge and deepen understanding in different contexts.

spiritual, moral, social and cultural development The curriculum of a maintained school must promote the spiritual, moral, cultural, social, mental and physical development of pupils. It is through these areas that schools play a dominant part in preserving social cohesion and values. They have a key responsibility in preparing pupils for the opportunities and difficulties surrounding adult life, the world of citizenship and the world of work. All pupils are required to attend a daily act of collective worship in schools, unless they are withdrawn by their parents. All schools must provide religious education as a part of the formal curriculum. An important way in which cultural development is promoted by schools is through *extra-curricular activities*, for example musical activities and residential and non-residential visits. It is the potential contribution of the whole school, its ethos, policies and curriculum provision, to pupils' all-round development which is difficult for parents to assess. OFSTED's inspection guidelines require inspection teams to report on this feature of a school's work and life. See *agreed syllabus; assembly; church schools; counselling; guidance; information; moral education; pastoral care; personal and social education (PSE); school visit; sex education; Standing Advisory Council on Religious Education (SACRE); Sunday school; tutor group; voluntary-aided schools; voluntary-controlled schools.*

split-site school This is a school which operates on two or more sites not on the same campus. Split sites often operate where two *secondary schools* were merged to make a single *comprehensive school*. A common solution, designed to minimise pupil travel between sites, is to designate one site as a *lower* and one as an upper school. See *high school.*

sports day This is a day of various athletic events, normally held in the summer term. Parents usually are invited and normally take part in the inevitable parents' race. There has been some debate over the restricted range of opportunities for children to take part in some sports days in which there may be a wholly competitive programme. In primary schools, and increasingly in secondary schools, it is becoming common to plan sports days which have maximum pupil participation as a prime objective.

staff appraisal See *appraisal.*

staff development   This is a term which relates to a school's policy for the planned development of its staff members' *skills* and *competences*. A plan for staff development will support an institution's strategic plan and arise from an individual member of staff's *appraisal* by his or her manager. It is likely to specify the use which will be made of school *closure days*, setting out a programme of *in-service education and training*. Larger schools will assign responsibility for staff development to a senior member of the *school management team*, often a deputy headteacher. Smaller schools, including most primary schools, will most often see responsibility for staff development as resting with the head. See *National Association for Staff Development (NASD)*.

staff meeting   This is a regular meeting of all the teachers in a school, normally chaired by the headteacher. Staff meetings are normally part of the teachers' contractual hours and so attendance is compulsory. They may be held at lunchtime but more often occur immediately after the close of the pupils' *school day*. Some staff meetings may also be arranged within a staff training or *closure day*. In secondary schools staff meetings will also be arranged on a *departmental* basis. The frequency of staff meetings is a matter for individual schools.

standard   The standard was a banner on a field of battle, a fitting emblem for an educational idea which is riven with controversy. Another origin of the idea of a standard was in the nineteenth-century *elementary* school where children moved through six 'standards', later seven, each of which was marked by certain expectations about pupil performance which were carefully measured by end of year *tests*. So the idea of a standard refers to the quality of the pupils' learning. It also, of course, refers to the quality of teaching. The widespread view that educational standards are falling, or in decline, is difficult to substantiate. Standards are not immutable or fixed. A decision not to continue the practice of long division need not mean that standards have fallen. Children may not be able to do long division but, arguably, it is more sensible for them to use a calculator. In other words standards and expectations change. Similarly a concern with quality of handwriting, or learning multiplication tables, or parsing sentences (i.e. to describe parts of sentences and words in grammatical terms) may be an indicator of the standard required or it may not. Standards need to be defined and criteria established. If the whole curriculum is about basic skills in English and maths then it is likely that children will have higher *attainment* levels in those areas than if they follow a more broadly-based programme; the most appropriate curriculum against which to judge is open to debate. See *Academic Audit Unit (AAU)*; *accountability*; *British Standard BS 5750*; *criterion-referenced test*; *Parents' Charter*; *quality*.

standard assessment tasks (SATs)   These are externally set tasks which pupils take at the end of a *key stage* of schooling, in other words when most children are 7, 11, 14 or 16. The idea for SATs originated in the report of the *Task Group on Assessment and Testing* (TGAT) set up in 1987 to advise on the *assessment* of the *National Curriculum*. It proposed a ten-level system of *testing* and drew a distinction between SATs and *teacher assessment* (TA). There were difficulties surrounding the early introduction of SATs in respect of some of the tasks themselves, which were designed as closely as possible to replicate normal classroom activities, and the amount of time teachers had to give to organising the activities and keeping records about them. The *Dearing* Report in 1993 responded to these difficulties by reducing and simplifying the SATs. It should be noted that the term 'standard assessment tasks' has tended to be superseded by 'standard assessment test', itself an illustration of the way the debate about National Curriculum assessment has proceeded.

standard deviation   This is a statistical term that can be used to show differences from the mean or average; the range of differences can be expressed as standard deviations. Average or mean scores alone are often insufficient for interpreting a full set of scores; it is important to know the extent to which scores 'scatter' (or deviate) from the average or mean. See *regression*; *standardised*; *Z-scores*.

Standard English   This is the received form of English which emphasises a basic *standard* in terms of grammatical construction, *spelling*, avoidance of local or colloquial expressions and a form of pronunciation, including *accent*, which makes the language accessible to all. It is wrongly taken to imply preference for an artificial form of southern, middle class, Oxbridge or BBC expression and this can lead to dispute about its relevance for all children. The *National Curriculum* acknowledges that Standard English is only one form of English, but it asserts that it is a form which children need in order to progress in the educational system and in their working and adult lives. See *basic skills*.

standard national scale (SNS)   This is the new arrangement for structuring teachers' pay. It is a single, 17-point scale which is intended to meet the needs of teachers with various responsibilities at different stages of their careers. It replaces the old structure of responsibility or incentive *allowances*.

standard number   This is a number, set by the *DFE*, which represents the minimum number of pupils which the admissions authority can admit to the relevant *year* group (assuming sufficient demand) in any academic year. It is permissible for admissions' authorities to admit in excess of the standard number. See *admission*.

standard spending assessment (SSA)   The assessment is a government device designed for imposing restraint on local community charges; through the SSAs, the government makes clear how funding will be determined for different areas of spending. The formula for determining the SSA for education is based on projected spending for the following phases: under-fives; primary; secondary; post-16; and others. See *budget; capitation; formula funding.*

standardised   There are two relevant definitions. The first is for a *test* that has unambiguous, standardised instruction for administering it; has been subjected to *pilot study*; adjusted for *validity* and *reliability* and which offers norms. The second definition concerns test scores; if the scores are standardised, then it should be possible to make comparisons with scores from other tests by using *Z-scores* or *standard deviation.*

Standing Advisory Council on Religious Education (SACRE)
In accordance with the 1988 *Education Reform Act* each *LEA* must establish a SACRE. The purpose is to advise on religious education and to determine where the legislative provisions for broadly Christian education and worship need not apply. Examples of the issues SACREs might consider are teaching methods, teaching materials and teacher training. See *agreed syllabus; spiritual, moral, social and cultural development.*

state boarding schools   There is a limited number of places available in state boarding schools, mainly for children whose parents are in the armed forces or children with particular needs or difficulties. The fees are normally paid by *LEAs*. See *boarding school; Service Children's Education Authority (SCEA)*. For further information contact:

State Boarding Information Service (STABIS)
Westmorland
43 Raglan Road
Reigate
Surrey
RH2 0DU

Telephone No: 01737 226450

state school   This term is used to distinguish publicly-funded, *maintained schools* from schools in the *independent sector*. State schools are funded by the government. If the school is part of the *local education authority* then funds come through the LEA. *Grant maintained schools* receive their funds direct from the *Funding Agency for Schools*. See *comprehensive school; National Curriculum; voluntary-aided schools*.

statement   This is a statement of a pupil's *special educational needs*. It is drawn up by the local education authority in order to determine the pupil's difficulties and the kind of individual support needed. The document is legally binding so the authority must ensure that needs are met. There is no legal obligation to give extra help to pupils who do not have statements. The first step in the statementing process takes place when the pupil with difficulties is assessed. Assessment is made by an *educational psychologist* who may involve other professionals, e.g. social workers, *speech therapists*. There is a legal obligation to involve parents at all stages before the statement, setting out the support for the pupil, is finalised by the LEA. See *diagnostic assessment; learning difficulty; remedial teaching; screening; school psychological service; special support assistants*.

statement of attainment (SOA)   A statement of *attainment* is a description of what a pupil will need to have achieved in order to be placed on a particular level within a given attainment target. In other words an SOA is a more precise objective than the broader *attainment targets* (ATs) of the *National Curriculum* as defined within the *statutory orders*. The SOAs are related to one of ten *levels of attainment* on a single continuous scale, covering all *key stages*. They are not used in art, music or physical education.

statutory order   This is a parliamentary device to ensure that certain powers given to ministers in legislation can be put into effect. In education, statutory orders are the means by which the provisions of the 1988 *Education Reform Act* in respect of the *National Curriculum* are put into effect. So, there are statutory orders concerned with each subject area of the National Curriculum. Statutory orders require the approval of parliament before they come into effect. See *non-statutory examples*; *non-statutory guidance*.

Steiner schools   Steiner schools take children of all school ages. The education provided is broadly Christian and holistic, based on the philosophy of Albert Steiner. For further information contact:

> Steiner Schools Fellowship
> Kidbrooke Park
> Forest Row
> East Sussex
> RH18 5JB
>
> Telephone No: 01342 82115

strand   This is a term sometimes used in connection with the *National Curriculum* to signify a sequence of ideas running through part of a subject. In National Curriculum terminology, a strand is a sequence of related *statements of attainment* which runs through several levels of an *attainment target* or parts of a *programme of study*.

streaming   This is a form of classroom organisation in which pupils are put into *classes* according to their general *ability*. They are then taught in those streamed classes for all subjects or courses. The use of streaming is controversial since parents worry that their children are in the wrong stream and begin to conform to expectations which may be too low for them. Most primary schools do not stream, preferring to use various forms of grouping arrangements within a mixed-ability class. Most secondary schools, similarly, prefer not to operate a policy of out and out streaming. Instead, they tend to use systems which involve various mixes of *banding* and *setting*.

structured play   These are planned opportunities for young children to engage in a variety of different kinds of *play* as a basis for learning.

student   A person who is undertaking study at further or higher education level is regarded as a student. There is now a growing tendency to substitute student for *pupil* (of compulsory school-age) so the old distinctions are being blurred.

student grant   See *grants*.

student union   In most colleges and universities, students belong to students' unions. A union usually encourages student societies for cultural activities, provides recreational, welfare and social facilities and nominates members to serve on official committees of the institution. See *National Union of Students*.

study skills   These are *skills* needed to undertake successful academic learning. In the primary school they include *reading* for information, using a library, using *IT*, undertaking investigations, and report writing. In secondary school there might be more emphasis on time management and various approaches to preparing for an *examination*. Study skills are needed at all ages and stages of education. Some may best be taught within the normal curriculum, others may benefit from discrete treatment within a study skills component.

summative assessment   This is a form of *assessment* which records the achievement of a pupil at the end of a given stage of education. The stage could be a project, a course unit, a term's work, a year's work, a *key stage* or the child's whole educational achievement. The term 'summative' indicates that the assessment is a 'summing up' which involves judgements about a child's learning. The term should be distinguished from *formative assessment*, which is ongoing, makes judgements about work in progress and is intended to help the teacher plan more effective learning for a child. But the more final, summative form of assessment need not imply a restricted approach to assessment. Nothing about summative assessment assumes a particular form of assessment such as formal examinations or paper and pencil tests. See *rank*; *Task Group on Assessment and Testing (TGAT)*.

Sunday school   Sunday schools became popular towards the end of the eighteenth century. The intentions behind them were to teach religion and morality to poor children who had to work every day (except Sunday). Some historians believe that Sunday school teaching was also intended to neutralise incipient, political radicalism. See *moral education*; *spiritual, moral, social and cultural development*.

supply teachers   These are teachers employed by a school to cover for teachers who are ill or unable to attend school for a variety of reasons, such as attendance on an *INSET* course or jury service. Most schools have contact with supply teachers who have built up a good working knowledge of the pupils, the teachers and school policies and routines.

support staff   This refers to non-teaching staff who support teachers in their work. Whilst the term can include administrative and secretarial support staff within the school, it more commonly refers to non-teaching assistants within the classroom. A variety of external support staff is also available, such as the *Education Welfare Officer* (EWO) and *educational psychologist*. See *ancillary staff; registrar; school secretary; Section 11 staff; special support assistants*.

support teachers   Support teachers give additional support for a variety of purposes. It could be for pupils with *special educational needs* or pupils for whom English is a second language. The support is most usually given within the child's own classroom, with the support teacher working alongside the child's class teacher. An alternative way of working is to withdraw the child from the class and to work elsewhere in a school with the child on an individual basis or in a small group. See *bilingual assistants; in-class support; language support teacher; learning support; peripatetic teachers; remedial teaching; Section 11 staff; special support assistants*.

syllabus   The syllabus is the programme to be followed in a subject area or group of subjects. It is difficult to distinguish from the term *curriculum* or *programme of study*. We could speak of a history syllabus, the Year 5 syllabus and the school syllabus in the same way as we could the history, Year 5 and school curriculum.

tables Multiplication tables are an approach to learning simple mathematical relationships. They can be learned by *rote*. It was the aspect of memorisation by rote or repetition which led some to criticise an undue emphasis on tables. In debate between traditionalist and progressive views in education, attitudes towards tables can be a potent symbol. With the increasing availability of calculators, it could be argued that it is less necessary than formerly for children to be good at recalling their tables. On the other hand, ready access to multiplication relationships is a helpful aid to mental calculation and, arguably, promotes mental agility. Unsurprisingly, the value of tables is seen as a part of a sensible back-to-basics educational policy. The vast majority of teachers teach them systematically, indeed there is little evidence to suggest that their use was ever abandoned. Undeniably, most parents regard children's knowledge of tables as a touchstone of effective schooling. See *memory*.

Task Group on Assessment and Testing (TGAT) The group was established in 1987 to advise the *Secretary of State* on the way in which *assessment* and *testing* would operate under the *National Curriculum*. Its chair was Professor Paul Black. The Task Group clarified the purposes of assessment, made distinctions between *formative* and *summative assessment*, and defined an approach which involved both *teacher assessment* (TA) and the use of *standard assessment tasks* (SATs). The Group also specified a ten-level scale for assessment and reporting, arguing that through the use of such a scale in each National Curriculum subject area learning and assessment would be seen as complementary, progressive and coherent. In the event the use of the ten-level scale has proved difficult in practice. It was a feature of the review of the National Curriculum by Sir Ron *Dearing* to which particular attention was paid.

teacher assessment (TA) This is the *assessment* of pupils' work by teachers throughout the *key stage*. It is undertaken by teachers as a normal part of their teaching. It should be distinguished from the *standard assessment tasks* (SATs) which are externally set, though marked by teachers. There has been continuing dispute about the relative weight that should be given to SATs and TA in assessing children's progress under the *National Curriculum*.

teacher–class ratio   The teacher–class ratio is determined by dividing the number of *full-time equivalent* (FTE) teaching staff by the number of *classes* in the school. The greater the ratio, the more teacher time is available for work other than direct teaching. See *contract ratio*; *free periods*; *non-contact time*.

teacher training   Teacher education and training is organised predominantly in *universities*, colleges and institutes of *higher education*. About 83 higher education institutions are involved in its provision. Approximately 24,000 students enter teacher training courses each year, half of them to join *undergraduate* routes and half the *Postgraduate Certificate in Education* (PGCE).

Government policy has been to develop a wider variety of training routes and to locate more training in schools. At the end of the 1980s schemes were announced to pilot new *articled teacher* and *licensed teacher* routes. The Articled Teacher Scheme was a two-year postgraduate course, mainly based in schools, which led to the award of the PGCE. The articled teachers had to be *graduates* over the age of 26. Licensed teachers did not have to be graduates and their courses of training were planned by individual schools, frequently in association with *LEAs*. Licensed teachers were granted a licence to teach over the two years of their training pending a recommendation to award *QTS*. The purpose was to break down the monopoly of *BEd* or BA/BSc (QTS) undergraduate courses and the PGCE. Recent policy initiatives have included the proposal to pilot *School-Centred Initial Teacher Training* (SCITT) where courses could be wholly school-based and do not necessarily involve higher education and the increasing involvement of the *Open University* in mounting the part-time PGCE. The overwhelming majority of teacher education students are still undertaking BEd and PGCE courses, however. In 1994 the Education Act established the *Teacher Training Agency* (TTA) to oversee policy development, funding and quality assurance. The TTA replaced the former advisory body in teacher training, the Council for the Accreditation of Teacher Education (CATE). See *block practice*; *bursary scheme*; *college of education*; *General Teaching Council (GTC)*; *higher degree*; *James Report*; *micro-teaching*.

Teacher Training Agency (TTA)   This new body was set up by the 1994 Education Act to oversee the system of teacher training in England and Wales. The eight to twelve members of the agency are appointed by the *Secretary of State* for Education and are responsible to him. The agency will receive reports from *OFSTED* on the quality of teacher training institutions. Decisions about funding levels will flow from this advice. An objective of the TTA is to establish more teacher training in schools, in part by encouraging the development of more *School-Centred Initial Teacher Training* (SCITT) schemes. The TTA replaced the Council for the Accreditation of Teacher Education (CATE), which was abolished in 1994. For further information contact:

Teacher Training Agency
Sanctuary Buildings
Great Smith Street
London
SW1P 3BT

Telephone No: 0171 925 3700

teachers   There are almost 400,000 teachers working in the maintained nursery, primary and secondary sectors. The overwhelming majority of these will have been trained through a formal higher education route to *qualified teacher status* (QTS), such as the Certificate in Education (CertEd), the *BEd* (or BA/BSc with QTS) or the *Postgraduate Certificate in Education* (PGCE). Recent changes have opened up new training possibilities, for example through the *licensed teacher* route, a controversial development since it challenged the notion of teaching as an all-graduate profession. The size of the teaching force has been one factor making it difficult for teachers to make gains in their professional status. There have been increasing calls to establish a *General Teaching Council* (GTC) as one way of advancing the professional standing of teachers, but there seems little prospect of immediate progress.

Teachers are employed by a school's governors. Advised by the head, governors determine how many staff and which staff should work at the school. Schools cannot employ as teachers persons deemed unsuitable by the *Secretary of State*. The governors determine the discretionary element of a teacher's pay, for example the starting salary. Teachers' pay scales are determined by an independent pay review body. All qualified teachers in *maintained schools* employed full-time (or at least 40 per cent full-time on contracts of not less than one year) are subject to appraisal of their performance on a two-year cycle. See *advisory teacher; articled teacher; coordinator; part-time teacher; peripatetic teacher; probationary year; supply teachers; support teachers; tutors*.

teachers' centres　These are centres organised and financed by *local education authorities* to act as locations for *in-service training* and places where resources can be consulted or borrowed. They are usually run by a warden, manager or centre leader appointed by the LEA. Most LEAs had a number of centres, so that teachers did not have too far to travel to use the service. The number of teachers' centres has been rapidly decreasing with the devolution of more money from LEAs to schools. See *local management of schools (LMS); resources for learning*.

teachers' ratings　These are the judgements which teachers make on the *coursework* of pupils. The judgements are normally expressed in terms of a mark or scale point. See *grades; group moderation; moderation*.

teacher's record book　This is a book which the teacher uses to plan and record teaching and learning for his or her class or classes on a regular basis. It is the scaffolding for a teacher's work and is often of necessity planned with other teachers in a team, for example a year group in a primary school. However the operation of the shared plan becomes the responsibility of an individual teacher.

teaching method　Teaching method describes the way in which a teacher organises the classroom, *instruction* and children so as to promote *learning*. It involves the teacher in making choices about method which may be influenced by the ages of the children, the subject matter and the availability of resources. It is concerned with the dimension of group size, whether the focus of instruction is a whole class, group or individual. It involves the dimension of resources, for example whether the basis of learning is book-based, dependent on IT or on a *workcard*. It involves a dimension concerned with the focus of learning, whether it is *child-centred*, giving children the opportunity to devise their own questions or investigations, or dominated by the teacher. Examples of teaching methods are lectures, or teacher instruction, question and answer, discussion, role play and simulation. See *direct method; look and say; pedagogy; phonics; problem-solving; programmed learning; reading; rote learning; seminar; spelling; teaching style*.

teaching practice　This term is generally used to describe periods when student teachers have an extended period of time in school so that they practice teaching skills. It is sometimes known as *block* *practice*. Extended periods of school teaching practice could be for as little as four or five weeks and as much as a whole term. Teaching practice could also occur for a day or two days a week for a number of weeks. In this case it is described as serial school experience or serial school practice.

teaching style   This term attempts to sum up a teacher's whole approach to teaching. A teacher's style may be judged by taking into account such factors as the *teaching methods* predominantly in use, the layout of the classroom, the teachers' attitude to reward systems and punishments, attitude to the teaching of tables and the character of social relationships in the classroom. Descriptions of teaching style commonly use the terms formal and informal or traditional and progressive, to represent opposite ends of a continuum of possible teaching styles. Alternative descriptions might be teacher-centred and *child-centred* or authoritarian and democratic. See *open-plan schools; ORACLE; passive learning; transmission teaching*.

team teaching   This is the teaching of a number of classes simultaneously by teachers operating in a team. The approach requires careful attention to planning, assessment and record-keeping. Teams will normally divide the work between them, allowing those with particular expertise to lead different parts of the work. The other members of the team would then be responsible for various kinds of follow-up work with classes, groups or individuals. See *teaching style*.

technical schools   The Spens Report on *secondary* education, published in 1938, recommended the provision of a *tripartite system* of *grammar*, technical and *secondary modern schools*. The 1944 Education Act introduced this system. Technical schools were intended to help promote the need for an applied engineering and scientific bias in the British educational system. See *bilateral school; Butler Act (1944 Education Act); multilateral education*.

Technical and Vocational Education Initiative (TVEI)   TVEI began as a pilot in 1983. It was an initiative of the Department of Employment, seeking to make the secondary curriculum more relevant to adult and working life. The scheme was for pupils aged 14 to 18 in full-time education, in schools and further education. It was managed by the *Manpower Services Commission* (MSC). The money spent under the initiatives was used to pay for additional teachers and a range of IT and technical equipment. The scheme is now managed by the local *Training and Enterprise Councils* (TECs). Funding is not currently planned beyond 1996. See *industry*; *training*; *vocational education*.

technological baccalauréat   This is a new form of baccalauréat with a specifically technological focus for students aged 16 and over. See *baccalauréat*.

technology   It is necessary to distinguish three uses of the term technology in schools:

- It is a part of the subject of *design and technology*, one of the *foundation subjects* of the *National Curriculum*.
- It is used in the term *Information Technology* (IT) to denote the work children undertake on computers in school.
- In a very general sense all schools and classrooms use a variety of technology, such as TV, video, audio tapes or overhead projectors (OHPs), to help promote pupil learning.

See *City Technology Colleges (CTCs)*; *National Council for Educational Technology (NCET)*.

tenure   Tenure refers to conditions under which academics' posts in *universities* are virtually guaranteed as a *sine qua non* of academic freedom. Employers, therefore, would have to show very clearly the grounds for dismissal. Under the *Education Reform Act (ERA) 1988* university rules and statutes governing tenure can be re-examined but changing existing conditions can be fraught with difficulty. Recent trends suggest that tenure is being weakened by the growing practice of offering short-term contracts for newly appointed staff.

term   The school year begins in September for most pupils and it is divided into three unequal terms. They are usually described by the season in which they take place, autumn, spring and summer, although some independent schools prefer ancient usages such as Michaelmas, Hilary and Lent. In higher education some institutions are moving to organise the academic year into two *semesters*, following the American pattern. See *half-term*.

tertiary college   The term denotes a college providing education in the third, or post-*secondary*, 16 to 19 phase. Tertiary colleges operate as *comprehensive* educational institutions, offering a wide variety of academic and *vocational* courses. They are firmly a part of the post-compulsory sector and operate a variety of *full-* and *part-time* courses.

They bring together courses which conventionally would be found in a school *sixth form* with courses which are commonly located in a *further education* college. They are seen by their supporters as a promising means of breaching the divide between the academic and vocational traditions in post-16 educational provision. See *Association for Colleges (AFC)*.

testing   This is a form of *assessment* which implies a formally pre-scribed task undertaken in formal conditions. The test is designed to assess the *quality* and extent of pupils' learning in relation to a par-ticular course or subject. Testing under the *National Curriculum*, for example, takes place at the end of each *key stage*, when children are aged 7, 11, 14 and 16. The means of testing is the *standard assessment task* (SAT). Testing is seen as an integral part of the government's approach to raising *standards* through the educational reforms of the late 1980s. It was planned that tests would give parents clear *informa-tion* about their children's progress in relation to commonly under-stood expectations. They would also allow judgements to be made about the relative effectiveness of schools as test results were pub-lished in the form of *league tables*. Thus, successful schools would attract pupils while unsuccessful schools would either improve under pressure from the market place or close down through a failure to attract pupils. The National Curriculum testing procedures led to ini-tial controversy when some of the tests were criticised by teachers in terms of their design, the interruption of children's entitlement to learning and the additional work-load they entailed for teachers. In 1993 the *Secretary of State* appointed Sir Ron *Dearing* to undertake a review of the National Curriculum and its associated testing proce-dures. Among the recommendations of the final Dearing Report (1993) were a simplification of the actual tests and a reduction in the number of areas to be tested. See *attainment; attainment test; criterion-referenced test; differential examination; difficulty index; examining; grades; intelligence quotient (IQ); item; multiple choice test; norm-referenced test-ing; objective test; pass mark; pass rate; performance test; profile component (PC); reliability; Task Group on Assessment and Testing (TGAT); validity*.

thesis   A thesis is a sustained piece of original research usually undertaken in the *university* sector as part of *postgraduate study* at Masters or Doctoral level. The end product is a lengthy report, the thesis, of up to 100,000 words. See *degrees; dissertation*.

three Rs   These are *reading*, writing and arithmetic. They were the staple of the *elementary* tradition in primary education and are still a powerful way of evoking the essence of traditional educational values. Much used in speeches of politicians eulogising a 'back to basics' approach, the narrowness and lack of excitement of a curriculum dominated by the three Rs is sometimes overlooked.

timetable   This is a plan of a school week. In a primary school this may or may not be organised into periods of instruction based upon subjects. It will, however, indicate when assemblies take place, when the school hall is to be used for PE, when school begins and ends and when breaks and lunch are taken. In a secondary school the day is generally broken up into defined periods, normally of 30–40 minutes. Subjects will be allocated to a number of individual or double-timetabled periods or slots. A full version of the secondary timetable, involving the allocation of teachers to all classes in the school and in all subjects, is a complicated piece of administration generally overseen by a deputy headteacher. Computer software is available to assist in the task. Some secondary schools' timetables are organised on a two-week cycle. See *after-school activities*; *block timetable*; *contact ratio*; *extra-curricular activities*; *free periods*; *school day*.

topic   A topic refers to work, usually in a primary school, which has a particular focus and is planned to last for a period of time, for example a week or half a term. Examples could include topics abut water, spring, ourselves, the high street or transport. The topic provides scope for work involving a number of subject areas and for investigative work by the children. The topic may involve a number of subjects in equal measure in an *interdisciplinary* way, or it may be led or dominated by a single subject (as in a history-led topic which also involves some consideration of mathematical, scientific, religious and geographic factors). The topic web is a schematic, annotated way of planning the topic, showing how a variety of ideas, activities, subject areas or skills are related to the core idea. The topic remains a favourite device by which primary schools teach aspects of the *National Curriculum*. Supporters of the approach argue that topic work has an established track record of capturing children's interest and enthusiasm, and that the best examples can promote very high-quality learning. Where topic work is weak, however, the result can be unfocused, repetitive work which does not really challenge children and about which there can be little certainty of the learning achieved. Topic work is sometimes described as *project* work or thematic work. See *integrated work*.

toy libraries Toy libraries lend toys in the same way as book libraries lend books. For further information contact:

Toy Libraries
Play Matters
68 Churchway
London
NW1 1LT

Telephone No: 0171 383 2714

training It is generally acknowledged that a better-trained workforce is needed, so that school leavers can make a strong contribution to national economic development. Training generally refers to courses designed to equip trainees with the skills required to do a job. The *Technical and Vocational Education Initiative* (TVEI) was designed to develop a more vocational curriculum in secondary and further education. *Youth Training* (YT) is an attempt to develop a national training entitlement. It is organised locally by the *Training and Enterprise Councils* (TECs). The system of training awards is being revised into a comprehensive system of *National Vocational Qualifications* (NVQs). See *Manpower Services Commission (MSC); Open College; vocational education.*

training days See *closure days; in-service education and training (INSET).*

Training and Enterprise Councils (TECs) These were established in 1991, taking on the role of the former *Manpower Services Commission* (MSC). There are more than eighty local TECs up and down the country. Their function is to distribute funds earmarked by the government for *Youth Training* (YT) in further education and schools. TECs are intended as the means by which all young people will develop skills for work and gain useful qualifications. They are dominated by the representatives of local business and industry. See *Technical and Vocational Education Initiative (TVEI); training.*

transition The term describes any movement of pupils – between classes, teachers and schools. The most common concern about transition is the effect on pupils of changing schools. There is a good deal of anxiety in this change, especially the move from *primary* to *secondary* school. Nowadays far more attention is paid to pupil needs at transition. Receiving schools, for example, may arrange for a secondary teacher to visit the pupils in their primary schools and to accompany them on a tour of their prospective secondary school in the term before they enrol. See *age of transfer; progression.*

transmission teaching   This is a style of teaching in which the emphasis is on transmitting *knowledge;* interaction in the classroom is dominated by the teacher, at the expense of pupils' participation. See *passive learning; teaching style.*

transport   Transport must be provided for children aged under eight when they live more than three miles from school. Free transport is not available where parents elect to send their children to more distant schools in preference to schools which are closer to home.

traveller education   Traveller education aims to provide access to and full integration in mainstream education for the children of travellers. The responsibility lies with *LEAs.* In some circumstances the education of travellers' children is undertaken by teachers visiting traveller sites. More commonly, travellers' children attend local schools. See *specific grants.*

travellers' children   These are the children of people who have a nomadic life-style, for example gypsy travellers, fairground or show people, bargees, circus families and New Age travellers.

tripartite system   This is the division of *secondary* education into three kinds of schools which characterised educational provision after the Second World War. The three types of schools were *grammar, technical* and *secondary modern.* The tripartite system was characterised by selection at 11+ to determine which children would go to grammar school. The system was gradually replaced by a *comprehensive* system during the 1970s. See *bilateral school; bipartite system; Butler Act (1944 Education Act).*

tripos   This is the term for an *honours degree* at the University of Cambridge.

trivium   The mediaeval school *curriculum* consisted of the trivium and the *quadrivium.* The trivium was made up of grammar, dialectic and rhetoric, the quadrivium of astronomy, geometry, music and arithmetic.

truancy   Truancy is unauthorised absence from school during the ages of 5 and 16 years, i.e. the period of compulsory schooling. In some areas, it is an intractable problem caused, it is thought, by *under-achievement* or boredom with certain teaching approaches and un-attractive learning environments. *Education Welfare Officers* (EWOs) are required to work closely with parents of persistent truants (*Children Act 1989*) in order to facilitate their early return to school. Truancy rates are now seen as a *performance indicator* (PI) of *school effectiveness*. See *league tables; Parents' Charter*.

tuck shop   This is a shop set up inside a school to sell snacks and drinks to children. It is usually run by the children themselves, with support from teachers, classroom assistants or volunteer helpers. The profits from school tuck shops are generally added to school funds, usually to buy additional items of equipment or stock. In some schools tuck shop profits are set aside to form a special fund to help children who would not otherwise be able to afford to go on school visits or residential field trips. Criticism may be levelled against the nutritional quality of fare available in some tuck shops.

tutor   This is a teacher who takes responsibility for the *pastoral* interests of pupils in a tutor or form group. The *form* tutor's responsibility is to oversee the pupils' general academic progress and to act as a counsellor when required. Tutors normally make an entry on the *reports* of pupils in their tutor groups which sums up general progress and comments on pupils' contribution to the life of the school, involvement in *extra-curricular activities, behaviour* and relationships with pupils and teachers. See *counselling; guidance; personal and social education (PSE)*.

tutor group   This is a term used in secondary schools to denote the grouping of pupils for registration and *pastoral care*. In the best practice tutors, or *form* teachers, will monitor and support the academic, personal and social progress of pupils in their groups. They will undertake planned activities to achieve these ends. See *house system; personal and social education (PSE); year system*.

~ U ~

underachievement This is a term used to describe a child who is achieving less at school than might be expected, given that child's *ability*. Underachievement, or underperformance, might lead a teacher to discuss the pupil's progress with parents, so that reasons can be established. Clearly a whole range of social, emotional and intellectual factors could help explain a child's underachievement. It may be considered in relation to individual pupil characteristics or in terms of the circumstances of defined groups (for example pupils from particular minority groups or economic backgrounds). See *deficit model; dyslexia; language deficit; late developers; Rampton Report; special educational needs (SEN)*.

undergraduate An undergraduate is a student in higher education who is studying for a first *degree*. See *graduate; honours degree*.

uniform It is a matter for individual governing bodies to determine policy about school uniform. After a move away from the wearing of uniforms in primary schools in the 1970s, there now seems to be a move back to it. Uniforms are generally favoured in primary schools, although all aspects of policy in this area can lead to difficulties as young people begin to assert their sense of individuality during adolescence. State sixth forms rarely adopt uniforms but independent schools are generally very keen on the idea for all their students. Some public school uniforms are still based on ancient tradition, such as those at Eton or Christ's Hospital, Horsham.

unions A number of trade unions are available to represent teachers' and headteachers' employment and professional interests. For further information contact:

National Union of Teachers (NUT)
Hamilton House
Mabledon Place
London
WC1H 9BD

Telephone No: 0171 388 6191

National Association of Schoolmasters and the Union of Women Teachers (NAS/UWT)
Hillscourt Education Centre
Rose Hill
Rednall
Birmingham
B45 8RS

Telephone No: 0121 453 6150

Association of Teachers and Lecturers (ATL)
7 Northumberland Street
London
WC2N 5DA

Telephone No: 0171 930 6441

Professional Association of Teachers (PAT)
2 St James's Court
Friar Gate
Derby
DE1 1BT

Telephone No: 01332 372337

National Association of Headteachers (NAHT)
1 Heath Square
Boltro Road
Haywards Heath
East Sussex
RH16 1BL

Telephone No: 01444 458133

Secondary Heads Association (SHA)
130 Regent Road
Leicester
LE1 7PG

Telephone No: 01533 471797

United Nations Educational, Scientific and Cultural Organisation (UNESCO)   This organisation, established in 1946, aims to foster international cooperation in social and educational spheres. Member nations are encouraged to participate in relevant programmes, e.g. emergencies, welfare, education. Britain withdrew from the Organisation in 1985. For further information contact:

UNESCO
7 place de Fontenoy
7532 Paris O7 SP
France

Telephone No: 00 33 1 45 68 10 00

Universities and Colleges Admissions Service (UCAS)   In 1992, the Universities Central Council on Admissions (UCCA) and the Polytechnics Central Admissions System (PCAS) were phased out and replaced by one body, UCAS. UCAS is responsible for administering the clearing system for places in higher education. For further information contact:

UCAS
PO Box 28
Cheltenham
Gloucestershire
GL50 3SA

Telephone No: 01242 222 444

university   This institution of *higher education* offers courses at *undergraduate* and *postgraduate* levels and is entitled to award its own *degrees* and *diplomas*. The first universities, Oxford and Cambridge, were established in the thirteenth century. During the nineteenth century, the number of universities increased and by 1902 there were colleges in at least ten cities, e.g. Birmingham, Leeds, Reading, Sheffield, Southampton. Further expansion took place after the Second World War and between 1961 and 1965 seven new universities – East Anglia,

Essex, Kent, Lancaster, Sussex, Warwick and York – were established. After the *Robbins Report* was published in 1963, nine colleges of advanced technology – Aston, Bath, Bradford, Brunel, Chelsea, City, Loughborough, Salford and Surrey – were granted university status. The abolition of the so-called *binary* divide between universities and polytechnics in 1992 greatly increased overall university provision. See *academic board; Association of University Teachers (AUT); binary system; chancellor; collegiate university; Committee of Vice-Chancellors and Principals (CVCP); credit; dean; delegacy; entrance awards; Further and Higher Education Act (1992); graduate; higher degree; Higher Education Quality Council (HEQC); honorary degree; honours degree; principal; professor; redbrick university; university entrance requirements; vice-chancellor.*

University Department of Education (UDE)   This department is usually responsible for *teacher training, in-service* courses and studies in education. See *Bachelor of Education (BEd).*

university entrance requirements   Applicants for *university* places are normally expected to have two *GCE A level* passes (minimum) in appropriate subjects. In practice, some university departments may prove more demanding while others may operate special entry procedures for non-standard or *mature* applicants. See *access course; matriculation; open admission.*

University of the Third Age (U3A)   The U3A in the United Kingdom was founded in 1982. Its members are retired citizens who wish to engage in educational activities in order to enrich their lives. The University is dedicated to providing a broad framework for the activities and is run by volunteers. See *adult education; continuing education.* For further information contact:

University of the Third Age
U3A National Office
1 Stockwell Road
London
SW9 9JF

Telephone No: 0171 737 2541

~ V ~

validation The term refers to a process of quality assurance through which a course or programme of study is deemed worthy of the validating body's seal of approval. In higher education, the validating body is the university. In further education validation may be arranged by bodies such as the Royal Society of Arts, Business and Technology Education Council or the City and Guilds of London Institute. It is common for various facets of a course, for example aims, philosophy, course structure and *assessment*, to be discussed by a panel appointed by the validating body and the team which will teach the course in the institution.

validity A term which is used to judge whether an educational test or measure is any good. A test is valid if it measures what it purports to measure. The idea is important and not straightforward. For example, an educational test may measure a child's comprehension skills rather than an ability to think or reason. Some tests may advantage certain populations of children rather than others because of the cultural assumptions implicit in the test. Tests of intelligence are interesting examples of the debates which can spring up about a test's validity. See *reliability*.

value added This is a term used to denote the extent to which a school or any other educational institution provides good value for children or students. The idea is that the effectiveness of schools should be based on comparisons of like with like. Thus, schools which share a similar pupil intake can be reasonably compared in terms of GCSE or A level examination performance. The school with a superior examination performance would have added more value to the performance of its children. The first attempts at producing government *league tables* of school performance were criticised because they did not attempt to measure value added. Instead, they compared like with unlike, producing a *rank* order of performance which was thought by some commentators to be of limited use. See *performance indicators (PIs)*; *school effectiveness*.

verbal reasoning   One of the two main approaches to measuring children's *intelligence quotient* (IQ) is the verbal reasoning test. The other main approach measures *spatial* awareness and ability. Tests of IQ were a principal means of testing at 11+ for selective secondary education. Verbal reasoning tests were standardised, *norm-referenced tests* which had been trialled among large samples. They were justified in terms of their *validity* and *reliability*, although criticisms were levelled against them because they appeared to favour children who had shared similar cultural experiences. Tests of verbal reasoning involve children in responding to a variety of written puzzles and word games.

vertical grouping   This is a way of grouping pupils in *classes* in which there is an age span of more than one year. Sometimes the term *family grouping* rather than vertical grouping is used. The use of vertical grouping is sometimes deliberately chosen as an educational preference. On occasions it may be that a school's particular mix of pupil ages, or small size, make it the only possible form of organisation. See *mixed-age class*.

vice-chancellor   The vice-chancellor is the chief executive officer of a *university*. See *Committee of Vice-Chancellors and Principals (CVCP)*.

village schools   Village schools are popular but expensive. They are small and because of changing demographic patterns they frequently have spare capacity. Because of their size and their traditional place as a focus of community life in the countryside, moves to close schools or amalgamate them with a neighbour are sometimes fiercely resisted. Small schools are comparatively expensive per capita since they require administrative support, management and the expense of building maintenance. They necessarily require teachers to share curriculum responsibilities among a small team and frequently employ vertical grouping as an organisational strategy. See *family grouping*; *school closure*; *small schools*. For further information contact:

Small Schools Network
School of Education
University of Exeter
Exeter
Devon
EX1 2LU

Telephone No: 01392 263263

viva   The viva voce examination, viva for short, is an *oral* examination of a candidate as part of the *assessment* procedures for an
award.

vocational education   Vocational education is organised to prepare pupils or students for working life. Traditionally, it has been
further education, rather than schools, which has been seen as the
main provider of vocational courses. The *Technical and Vocational
Education Initiative* (TVEI) was designed to make the secondary school
post-14 curriculum more vocational in focus. Vocational education is
designed to prepare pupils for the workplace by giving them appropriate *skills* or *competences*. The government is anxious to develop a
national approach to vocational qualifications through a system of
National Vocational Qualification (NVQs). These build on the work of
the *City and Guilds, BTEC* and other vocational awards. See *Certificate
of Pre-Vocational Education (CPVE); Diploma of Vocational Education
(DVE); General National Vocational Qualification (GNVQ); link course;
National Council for Vocational Qualifications (NCVQ); Open College;
Ordinary National Certificate (ONC); Ordinary National Diploma (OND);
practical assessment; Royal Society of Arts (RSA); sandwich course; tertiary
college; training.*

voluntary-aided schools   These are state schools which are partly
funded by the church. About 85 per cent of the funding still comes
from the *LEA*. The main difference with a voluntary-aided school is
that it has a religious policy which gives emphasis to a particular religious tradition. The church appoints two thirds of a voluntary-aided
school's governing body. See *church schools; dual system; maintained
schools; spiritual, moral, social and cultural development.*

voluntary-controlled schools   These schools have no funding
from the church but have a close relationship with the church. All
the funding for voluntary-controlled schools comes from the *local education authority.* See *church schools; dual system; maintained schools; spiritual, moral, social and cultural development.*

Voluntary Service Overseas (VSO)   The idea of VSO is to help promote a range of services in the developing world. Several hundred people, many of them having just completed university degrees, join various educational, social and economic projects overseas each year. The intention is to stimulate development activity in the host country. For further information contact:

> Voluntary Service Overseas
> 317 Putney Bridge Road
> London
> SW15 2PN
>
> Telephone No: 0181 780 2266

vouchers   In an educational context vouchers are associated with the ideas of the radical right. They are seen as a way of giving *parents* more responsibility and choice over the education they select for their children, on the one hand, and as making schools more responsive and accountable to parents on the other. Parents would receive a voucher entitling them to educational services worth a prescribed sum of money for each child of school age. The voucher would then be cashed in by the parent when educational services were purchased. The parents' educational requirements and specifications would be the key determinant, leading schools to respond more and more to parents' wishes. The purpose is to promote an educational market place. There have been limited experiments with vouchers, especially in post-compulsory education. So far moves to introduce vouchers into mainstream provision within the compulsory years of schooling have been resisted.

~ WXYZ ~

Warnock Report   This was the report of the committee of inquiry, chaired by Mary Warnock, which investigated the education of children and young people with learning handicaps. It reported in 1978. Among its recommendations were that children with learning problems should be seen as having *learning difficulties* and not referred to as requiring *remedial* help. It was proposed that consideration of children with *special educational needs* should be a part of all courses of initial teacher education. The most critical proposal was that educational provision for children with learning difficulties should be integrated within the mainstream classroom, and not take place in specially formed remedial classes. The report contended that about 20 per cent of children in a class were likely to have one form or another of special educational need. There was a White Paper on 'Special Needs in Education' and an Education Act in 1981 which put many of the Warnock Committee's proposals into the statute book.

weighting   This is a technical term in *assessment* which concerns the contribution of elements of assessment to a candidate's overall result.

welfare assistants   The term describes the role of *classroom assistants* who help teachers working with pupils with *special educational needs*. At the moment welfare and classroom assistants have no teaching qualifications. In 1994 the government undertook a process of consultation and invited bids from organisations interested in mounting pilot schemes for the training of specialist classroom assistants. See *ancillary staff; specialist teacher assistants (STA)*.

Welsh Office Education Department (WOED)   Schools in Wales are subject to the same education legislation as those in England. The Welsh language is compulsory for all pupils, although the provision of it varies in Welsh-speaking and non-Welsh-speaking schools. Primary and secondary education is the responsibility of the Secretary of State for Wales. See *Curriculum and Assessment Authority* *for Wales (ACAC); Secretary of State; Welsh-speaking schools*. For further information contact:

Welsh Office Education Department (WOED)
Government Buildings
Ty Glas Road
Llanishen
Cardiff
CF4 5WE

Telephone No: 01222 761456

Welsh-speaking schools   In Welsh-speaking schools more than half the basic curriculum subjects, other than English or Welsh, are taught wholly or partly through the medium of the Welsh language.

White Paper   The expression is used because of the colour of this kind of official document. White Papers are issued as authoritative guides to government thinking, sometimes allowing time for consultation and negotiation, as part of the process of developing legislation for parliament.

whole curriculum   The whole curriculum of a school incorporates the basic *curriculum* and all other curricular provision. The point is made that excessive concentration on individual subjects can lead to a failure to see the links and interconnections between different curriculum areas. A concern with the impact of the whole curriculum on a child will consider such issues as *breadth*, depth, *progression*, continuity and relevance. The approach to whole curriculum planning adopted by the *National Curriculum Council* was criticised on the grounds that it failed to establish principles for the whole curriculum before setting up a series of subject working groups which reported their recommendations separately. See *cross-curricular*.

withdrawal   This refers to the removal of pupils with particular needs from class teaching in the primary school and from specified subjects in secondary schools. Help for these pupils is provided individually or in small groups. Withdrawal is sometimes criticised on the grounds that it isolates children and draws attention to their difficulties. In many cases a policy of providing special help within the child's own classroom is preferred. See *remedial teaching; special educational needs (SEN); support teachers*.

work experience　This is an opportunity for *secondary* pupils to have experience of the world of work for one or two weeks. It normally takes place during term time as a planned part of a pupil's education. The pupil will work as a kind of employee in a place of work, carrying out a particular job or range of tasks. Work experience introduces pupils to aspects of the environment and discipline of employment. It is accompanied, in the best schemes, by careful preparation and follow-up, so that the educational aspects of the experience are emphasised. See *business education; Compact; industry*.

workcard　A workcard is a way of giving children instructions about a task to be completed. It normally includes some material (text, diagram, photograph) which is central to the task. The workcard may be part of a set which deals with a *topic* or area of study in a systematic way, or it may be an individual task which stands alone. Workcards may be devised by a teacher, perhaps to meet the needs of particular children, or they may be commercially obtained. Over-reliance on workcards is sometimes criticised as leading to over-prescriptive and potentially unimaginative teaching. They are, however, a useful way of responding to individual children's circumstances and learning requirements. See *teaching method*.

Workers' Education Association (WEA)　The Association was founded in 1903 to promote the education of workers. It originally involved the universities and trade unions in partnerships to provide appropriate courses for working people, predominantly male trade unionists and supporters of the Labour Party. Its original mission became somewhat diluted in the post-Second World War period when the advantage of WEA courses was taken largely by the middle class. It remains a significant provider of locally available *adult education*. See *continuing education*. For further information contact.

Workers' Education Association
17 Victoria Park Square
London
E2 9PB

Telephone No: 0181 983 1515

World Education Fellowship　See *New Education Fellowship*.

year system　The year system is a structure for *pastoral care* and pupil welfare within a school, normally a secondary school. All children are grouped according to years. The pastoral system is usually organised into *tutor* or registration groups overseen by *form* tutors and the head of year. See *banding; house system; mixed-ability class; setting; streaming.*

youth service   The service is responsible for providing social, cultural and leisure activities for people between the ages of 11 and 25. It is organised by local education authorities. See *Community Service Volunteers (CSV); National Youth Agency.*

Youth Training (YT)   Various schemes of Youth Training have been in existence since 1983. The current scheme, organised by the *Training and Enterprise Councils* (TECs), provides work-based *training* for people aged 16 to 25. When training, participants are paid the same as they would receive if they were claiming unemployment benefit. Since young people under the age of 18 are no longer entitled to unemployment benefit, YT is almost compulsory for some 16- to 18-year-olds.

Z-scores   These are *standarised* scores derived by considering the differences between actual and mean scores. Differences are usually given in terms of the *standard deviation*. For example, actual scores below the average would be calculated as minus Z-scores but scores about the mean score calculated in units of standard deviation would have plus Z-scores. See *regression.*

zero budgeting approach   In this approach to budgeting, the principles and priorities of previous *budgets* are set aside and *head-teacher, bursar* and *governors* begin with a clean sheet. The approach can be used effectively when the school wants to implement a new school *development plan.*

GOLDMINE

Finding free and low-cost resources for teaching

1995–1996

Compiled by David Brown

"It can be highly recommended because the choice of subjects, the organisation of the entries, and an index make a mass of information very easily accessible. Having used this directory to acquire resources for a couple of ad hoc topic areas, I can confidently state that it works - with ease and practicability. In the saving of teachers' time, let alone in access to materials, it really is a goldmine. I would advise any school to acquire this book. The title of the book is wholly accurate and the outlay is modest compared with the returns." **School Librarian**

David Brown has been teaching in primary, middle and secondary schools for 23 years. It was through David's need to find resources within a limited school budget that he began to uncover a wealth of low-cost, good quality material which was just what he was looking for.

Goldmine places these resources into topic areas, describes them and tells you where you can get them from. Since the first edition in 1985, **Goldmine** has developed into the country's leading directory of free and sponsored teaching resources, providing the wherewithal to obtain over 6000 resources from some 235 supliers.

Budget-conscious schools will find it saves its purchase price many times over, and parents and teachers are safe in the knowledge that all the items described in here ar personally recommended by a teacher, the compiler himself.

1995   329 pages   1 85742 137 X   £15.00

Price subject to change without notification

50 POPULAR TOPICS

A resources directory for schools

Compiled by David Brown

You are resourcing a topic, and you don't know who publishes what. The school doesn't have all the publishers catalogues you need, and you don't have addresses for those you haven't got.

THE RESOURCES DIRECTORY has been compiled to solve all these problems. The 50 most popular primary and secondary school topics are included with a huge range of books, videos, software, kits, packs, equipment and schemes for all ages between 5 and 13.

Over 2500 items from 50 suppliers are included, together with their addresses, all grouped in topics, cross-referenced in a comprehensive index and with an appendix of schemes in science, technology, geography and history.

David Brown is a schoolteacher with over 20 years teaching experience in primary, middle and secondary schools. He is also author of 'GOLDMINE', published by Arena.

1995   201 pages   1 85742 163 9   £15.00

arena

CONCISE GUIDE TO

Customs of Minority Ethnic Religions

David Collins
Manju Tank
Abdul Basith

Much has been written on the subject of Community Relations. This small book does not claim to add to this knowledge, but rather to distil it in a brief, orderly, and accessible form for the everyday reader, who needs basic guidance for the purposes of everyday work. It makes no assumptions about existing understanding or interest on the part of the reader, and aims to enable readers to meet the needs of minority ethnic consumers in a more sensitive and respectful way.

The Guide contains basic useful information on Judaism, Sikhism, Hinduism, Islam, Buddhism/Taoism/Confucianism, and Rastafarianism. Each section is divided into modules dealing with Symbols, Languages and Scripts, Names, Beliefs, Prayer, Religious Festivals, Dress, Diet, Medical Treatment, Social Rules, Birth Customs and Visiting.

1993   84 pages   1 85742 120 5   £5.50

Price subject to change without notification

— *The* —
LEGAL RIGHTS
Manual

SECOND EDITION

A guide for social workers and advice centres

Jeremy Cooper

This book provides social workers, advice centres and those engaged in caring for others, together with their clients, with an up-to-date body of information and advice on their legal rights, covering a wide range of areas and activities.

Written in a concise, non-technical and readable style the book describes how individuals and groups can use the law to their advantage in a diverse range of settings, including: housing, the workplace; living with mental or physical disability, dealing with council and other public officials, problems with the police, living with old age, and as a consumer of goods and services. It also provides the reader with a mass of information on where to go for further advice and assistance in each of these areas. This fully updated and revised second edition states the law as it stands on 1 March 1994.

Jeremy Cooper is a barrister and Professor of Law and Head of the Law Division at the Southampton Institute.

1994   319 pages   1 85742 136 1   £19.95

Price subject to change without notification

arena